Robert Bell is a financial services compliance consultant, owner and founder of RB Compliance Consultancy Ltd since 2012. Before that he held senior compliance roles in financial services firms and a Solicitors' practice.

Robert has authored industry recognised guidance in relation to vulnerability and GDPR, and lectures on compliance subjects for a range of organisations.

A Practical Guide to the Financial Conduct Authority (FCA) Consumer Duty

A Practical Guide to the Financial Conduct Authority (FCA) Consumer Duty

Robert Bell LLB
RB Compliance Consultancy Ltd

Law Brief Publishing

Published 2024 by Law Brief Publishing, an imprint of Law Brief Publishing Ltd
30 The Parks
Minehead
Somerset
TA24 8BT

www.lawbriefpublishing.com

Paperback: 978-1-916698-44-4

For Lucy and all those who have helped me, especially my wife Isabelle.

PREFACE

The Financial Conduct Authority (FCA) have created a complex set of standards which fundamentally change the way organisations interact with customers, moving from a generalised approach to one aligned with the needs of those in the target market. The FCA provides a standardised method to achieve compliance, a product governance framework which is set out in PRIN 2A. Those working in financial services must understand the key components of this governance framework, in particular how it impacts their role/firm.

Moreover, the way in which firm's interact with each other has shifted. Manufacturers and Distributors are expected to have a closer relationship, one where customer feedback and outcomes are shared in order to support the Manufacturer in their development of the product or service. The Manufacturer is expected to use this information to create guardrails which must be followed by Distributors as well as their own staff.

It's clear the Consumer Duty has changed the way organisations function in the financial services market. However, as with any new set of regulatory requirements, ascertaining exactly what needs to be done can be a challenge. This book represents the law up to 31st May 2024 and aims to provide detail where ambiguity exists.

Robert Bell
July 2024

CONTENTS

CHAPTER ONE

INTRODUCTION

1.1: About this book

This book is about compliance with the Consumer Duty as set out by the Financial Conduct Authority (FCA) in their Policy Statement 22/9, Final Guidance 22/5 and subsequent interventions up to and including the first quarter of 2024. It aims to highlight the greatest challenges that UK financial services firms have in implementing the Duty and presents key requirements in a way that is understandable for most readers. However, this book has been written on the assumption that the reader is already familiar with the Consumer Duty. As such it is focused on the more intricate, and therefore interesting, aspects of the Duty.

Terms defined in the FCA Handbook have the same meanings in this book. All publications referenced are published by the FCA unless otherwise specified. These include webpages and 'documents' such as Dear CEO letters, reports, investigations and enforcement action. Other types of FCA publication include Consultation Papers (CP), Discussion Papers (DP), Finalised Guidance (FG), Market Studies (MS) Policy Statements (PS) and Thematic Reviews (TR), where, in each case, the first two digits of the reference number are the publication year.

1.2: A Failure of Treating Customers Fairly

The FCA and Prudential Regulation Authority (PRA) were created following the 2008 financial crisis, also known colloquially as the credit crunch. Following a period of review by the Government elected in 2010 the Financial Services Act 2012 was passed, and the new regulatory regime was born.

Under the 'twin-peaks' model, the FCA is mainly concerned with the conduct of regulated firms whilst the PRA regulates the 1,500-2,000 firms undertaking higher risk activities, focusing on market stability. Both regulators began work in April 2013 with the FCA, in particular, acquiring its regulatory standards from the previous regulator, the Financial Services Authority (FSA).

Treating Customers Fairly (TCF) is one of the more well-known set of standards inherited by the FCA. Originally created by the FSA in 2006, the TCF initiative was continued by the FCA, with the new regulator embedding the six TCF outcomes in the sixth principle of businesses "Customers interests – A firm must pay due regard to the interests of its customers and treat them fairly".[1]

However, during the tenure of both regulators, industry research has found instances of practices inconsistent with the TCF principles. The mis-selling of Payment Protection Insurance (PPI) highlights one of the more egregious examples of financial services firms prioritising income over customer needs or outcomes and therefore failing to treat customers fairly. This example also emphasises the role that different firms in the distribution chain can play in failing to treat customers properly. One tends to blame the introducer (the firm selling the product to the customer, often a retailer) for mis-selling, an understandable assumption as they were often the party disguising the true cost of the insurance, failing to check whether it was suitable and sometimes even signing on behalf of customers. However, the manufacturer (the insurer) was often at fault as well due to a failure in oversight and control of the distributor's actions or knowingly allowing them to conduct such practices.

Poor practices were not limited to PPI, with several instances across a range of markets including poor affordability assessments undertaken by several high-cost-short-term-credit (HCSTL, otherwise known as payday loan) providers. This often resulted in customers borrowing again, or

---

1 PRIN 2.1 The Principles – FCA Handbook

rolling over their loan, so the amount of credit borrowed grows – profitable for the lender but trapping the customer into a cycle of debt. Of course, there is also the expense of HCSTC loans. Payday lenders have been singled out as charging very high interest rates, which have been justified in part by the lenders due to the relatively small amount of credit involved and the risk to the firm, given that the customer base includes a large proportion of customers with low financial resilience. The FCA has, however, also criticised the high charges in unauthorised overdraft fees and the rent-to-own sector, among others.

Insurance pricing practices were criticised by the FCA in the General Insurance Pricing Practices Market Study (MS18/1.3)[2] for several reasons including 'price walking', the practice of charging loyal customers more to take advantage of a behavioural bias – inertia – where customers prioritise convenience and it is less likely that they will switch to a lower priced product. This and other failures led the regulator to believe that TCF had failed, and a new, stronger set of standards were required – which would form the Consumer Duty.

1.3: The Scope of the Duty

The importance of the Duty to the financial services industry is encapsulated by its wide scope; the Duty applies to all firms in the distribution chain where they have a material impact on the outcomes received by customers. However, there are a number of factors to take into consideration.

Regulatory perimeter

In its Final Guidance FG22/5 the FCA confirmed that the scope of the Duty is limited to the regulatory remit of the FCA meaning only firms conducting activities in the UK are in-scope. This means that only firms

---

2 MS18/1.3: General insurance pricing practices: Final Report (fca.org.uk)

holding FCA permission, or temporary permissions under the post-Brexit temporary permissions regime, are subject to the Duty. It is accepted that in some cases it will mean the Duty does not apply to some firms in the distribution chain.

It should be noted that where the distribution chain involves a company operating out of Gibraltar, the Duty still applies. At the time of writing the aim is for a Gibraltar Authorisation Regime (GAR) to be established. This will enable UK market access for specified financial services firms and it is expected that the GAR will align its rules with the FCA's.

The Duty generally only applies to activity under the FCA's supervision, therefore activity falling outside of their remit, such as unregulated business lending, is not subject to the Duty.

Some unregulated activity can fall within the scope of the Duty. Where an unregulated activity is required as part of the delivery of a regulated activity (i.e. an ancillary activity) then it will be subject to the Duty. However, the sale of an unregulated product, separate and distinct from the regulated product, even if sold at the same time, is not subject to the Duty.

Retail Market Business

Principle 12 and 2A apply to a firm's retail market business in respect of both open and closed products. In this case, the term 'retail market business' means products and services which are offered to 'retail customers'. The FCA has chosen to align the definition of retail customers with the FCA Handbook, it therefore differs depending on the sector the organisation operates in. The FCA offer the following summary in FG 22/5:

- For consumer credit, the Duty applies to all regulated credit-related activities.

- For deposit-taking activities, the Duty applies to consumers, micro-enterprises, charities with a turnover of less than £1 million and a natural person acting in a capacity as a trustee if acting for purposes outside their trade, business or profession (in line with the 'banking customer' test in the Banking Conduct of Business Sourcebook (BCOBS)).

- For insurance, the scope follows the position in the Insurance Conduct of Business Sourcebook (ICOBS). The Duty does not apply to reinsurance, contracts of large risk sold to commercial customers or other contracts of large risk where the risk is located outside the UK. Nor does it apply to activities connected to the distribution of group insurance policies or the extension of these policies to new members.

- For investments, the Duty applies to business conducted with a customer who is not a professional client, as set out in the Conduct of Business Sourcebook (COBS).

- For mortgages, the Duty follows the position in the Mortgage Conduct Business Sourcebook (MCOB). The Duty therefore applies to all regulated mortgage contracts within the perimeter but not, for example, unregulated buy-to-let contracts or commercial lending. Where the owner of a mortgage book is unregulated and the regulated party is an administrator, the Duty would apply in an appropriate and proportionate manner to the administrator's function.

- For payment service or e-money providers, the Duty applies to business conducted with consumers, micro-enterprises and small charities (where the definitions of these terms are the same as for deposit takers, as noted above).[3]

It is, then, clear that the scope of the Duty goes beyond customers who have purchased or used a product or service. Firms providing information to or answering questions of a prospective customer, handling an application or even a complaint, will need to comply with the Duty.

It is more difficult to ascertain whether financial promotions are within the scope of the Duty in so far as they don't necessarily result in the onboarding of a retail customer. Therefore, the test which must be applied, under PRIN 3.2.6, is whether the promotion is likely to be received by a retail customer.

Where products are sold to both retail and non-retail customers, and it is impossible for the firm to separate the two in the design or delivery of that product, the FCA have confirmed that the Duty should be applied and, in this situation, products sold to non-retail customers are not excluded.

Distribution chain

Throughout the Duty the terms 'distribution chain', 'manufacturer' and 'distributor' are used repeatedly. The purpose of the regulator's use of the terms is to make it clear that adherence to the Duty is not reliant on the organisation having a direct relationship with the retail customer, instead any organisation which has a material impact on the service received by the retail customer falls within scope.

The FCA define the distribution chain as "from product and service origination through to distribution and post-sale activities. By the 'distribution chain', we mean all firms involved in the manufacture, provision, sale and ongoing administration and management of a product or service to the end retail customer" (FG 22/5). Only those who do not

[3] https://www.fca.org.uk/publication/finalised-guidance/fg22-5.pdf p.8

have a 'material influence' will be out of scope. Firms that have a material influence are those which determine the design or operation of retail products or services, including their price and value, distribute the product or service, prepare and/or approve communications that are to be issued to retail customers, or those that engage in customer support for retail customers.

See Chapter 2 for further information on the different roles in the distribution chain.

Wholesale markets

The FCA, in Final Guidance FG22/5 state "the Duty applies to all firms that can determine or have a material influence over retail customer outcomes. This could include firms in the wholesale market, even if they do not have a direct relationship with retail customers."[4]

Instead, firms need to look at their role in designing products. A wholesaler that creates a structured product for distribution in the market will fall under the scope of the Duty, whereas one that provides only elements of a product, which are then pieced together by an independent third party to form a product, will not be subject.

In the guidance document the FCA lists the following as excluded from the Duty:

- Manufacture of products or services only for wholesale purposes, where they meet the conditions in the 'retail market business' definition.

- Activities relating to non-retail financial instruments.

[4] https://www.fca.org.uk/publication/finalised-guidance/fg22-5.pdf p.15

- Market activities for certain financial instruments meeting the criteria in the 'retail market business' definition.

- Activities relating to insurance contracts of large risks for commercial customers or where the risk is located outside the UK.

- Activities connected to the distribution of group insurance policies or the extension of these policies to new members.

- The regulated activity of administering a benchmark, any ancillary activity to that activity and any activities undertaken by a benchmark administrator for the purpose of complying with the Benchmarks Regulation.[5]

Other points to note

While the Duty is not retrospective in so far as it does not apply to activities that took place prior to July 2023, it does apply to products and services already created and sold to customers or those still on sale. Such products are captured by the product review requirement under the products and services outcome, this will be explained in later chapters.

Where the manufacturer or distributor are already subject to product governance requirements those requirements will continue, the Duty does not intend to over-ride such requirements. For example, PRIN 2A.3.1G states "The product governance obligations on firms under Principle 12 are general in nature and should be considered alongside any other legal or regulatory obligations that may apply, for example any marketing restrictions in relation to the product". In other words, the Duty applies *in addition* to existing requirements,

5 https://www.fca.org.uk/publication/finalised-guidance/fg22-5.pdf p.15

and will not impact on those requirements, although the firm will need to ensure the expectations of the Duty are fully met.

CHAPTER TWO

DEFINITIONS

2.1: Introduction

The Consumer Duty created a small number of new definitions which must be understood to be able to properly comprehend the requirements. This chapter explains those key definitions, and this book is structured to highlight the manufacturers' requirements separately to the distributors', where appropriate.

2.2: Manufacturers

Manufacturers are the central player in the Duty, they are the organisations that create a product or service which is distributed to a retail customer. They are defined as a firm which "(a) creates, develops, designs, issues, manages, operates, carries out, or (for insurance or credit purposes only) underwrites a product; or (b) in relation to a closed product or an existing product:

(i) created, developed, designed or issued the product; or

(ii) manages, operates, carries out, or (for insurance or credit purposes only) underwrites the product."

(FCA Handbook)

2.3: Distributors

Distributors are those working to deliver the product to the customer, either through direct relationships with customers (such as IFAs or brokers) or those acting as a 'step' within the chain. They are formally defined as "a firm which offers, sells, recommends, advises on, arranges, deals, proposes or provides a product".[6]

2.4: Co-manufacturers

In FG 22/5 the FCA state that there "may be multiple manufacturers for a single product or service. For example, an intermediary might design an investment fund and work with a fund manager to launch it. Both are considered co-manufacturers." (FG 22/5). The test is whether a firm can materially influence the design of a product or service. For example, where a firm helps another to determine the target market, or key features such as the operation of the service, or cost or limitations, then they are likely to be considered to be a co-manufacturer. A further useful test is whether the organisation is carrying out any of the assumed functions of the manufacturer such as signing-off a product or service or determining its terms and conditions.

Where a co-manufacturer relationship exists, both firms must have a written agreement in place setting out their respective roles and responsibilities. It must ensure the Duty is met, between both parties, in full, and that accountability is clear.

2.5: Supplier

Where firms operate solely on the mandate of another firm in the distribution chain and do not otherwise meet the definition of a distributor or manufacturer, such as IT providers, they can be designated a 'supplier', in which case the Duty will not apply.

---

6 https://www.handbook.fca.org.uk/handbook/glossary/G3563d.html?date=2104-01-01

2.6: Open Products

An open product is not defined within the final rules or guidance, other than to say it is a product which is not a closed product. In practice, given the definition of closed products, the term 'open product' is likely to denote products that are currently available for purchase and are marketed and distributed to retail customers.

2.7: Closed Products

The FCA Handbook defines closed products as:

> "(1) where there are existing contracts with retail customers entered into before 31 July 2023; and
>
> (2) which is not marketed or distributed to retail customers (including by way of renewal) on or after 31 July 2023."

CHAPTER THREE

PRODUCT GOVERNANCE

3.1: The Product Governance Framework

The Duty is often visually represented through a triangle with the four outcomes at the base, cross-cutting rules in the middle and the principle sitting on top, signifying its position as the over-arching prerequisite to compliance. However, the Duty is best understood through inverting this triangle and considering the outcomes first, followed by the cross-cutting rules and finally the principle. This is because the four outcomes provide us with the tangible practical steps which must be taken to comply and whilst firms undertake these steps, the cross-cutting rules are applied.

To aid understanding, a helpful starting point is the following brief example. PRIN 2A.3 requires manufacturers to have a product approval process. The requirements of PRIN 2A.3 are fairly prescriptive in so far as they require firms to identify the target market for the product (who it will be designed for), the characteristics of those in the target market (such as financial experience, education level, financial life stage and vulnerabilities), the proposed nature of the product or service, and why it can be beneficial for the target market. To understand this last point, firms must assess their customers' financial objectives, determine which customers the product can help to achieve their goals, and use this analysis to identify the steps that can be taken to ensure the product reaches the intended customer profile; this is the distribution strategy.

During the product approval stage, it is also essential to review the product against the other cross-cutting rules. Foreseeable harm is the most important of the cross-cutting rules. This is where the manufacturer, as part of the approval process, will identify the customers who are likely to be harmed by the product and therefore design the distribution strategy in a way to avoid, where possible, marketing of the product reaching these customers. It is not possible to avoid harm to customers solely by avoiding certain segments of customers; harms can occur to all customers for a range of reasons. Such harms may materialise due to several factors including changes in the customer's circumstances (e.g. loss of job leading to mortgage arrears or early retirement due to ill health leading to the need to access cash savings earlier) and external changes (e.g. economic changes leading to an increase in the interest rate paid by the customer). Manufacturers are also required to design the service to manage these identified harms, or, if possible, avoid them all together. Once identified, the manufacturer is obliged to design the product in a way that reduces the overall harm to the customer, should one of these events occur. Foreseeable harm goes further than events and we will explore this in subsequent chapters.

When designing the product, the manufacturer must ask itself whether it is designing the product in good faith, the final cross-cutting rule. Again, this should be recorded in the product approval document. For example, the manufacturer should be reviewing whether the product's features have been designed with the customer's needs in mind or simply to reduce costs or increase income without concern as to whether any additional features would significantly improve the customer's experience, even at the cost of the firm. Put simply, products shouldn't be designed solely with profit in mind. Whilst profit and sustainability are important, the needs of the customer must be equally considered when designing the key features.

In this example you can see how the cross-cutting rules apply to one element of the outcomes, the product approval process. The same process applies to open and closed product reviews and value assessments where the cross-cutting rules form part of the assessments.

The communication and customer service outcomes act almost as a bridge between the product approvals, product reviews and value assessments to the cross-cutting rules. Good, clear communication is a tool which is necessary to ensure the product reaches the correct target market and to help customers attain their financial objectives. For example, a manufacturer may identify a key characteristic of those in the target market as low reading age. Therefore designing (and testing) communications so that they are understandable to for customers with a low reading age can help to ensure that they are provided with the right information to be able to make an informed decision on their purchase and use of the product.

Consumer support, in much the same way, is an essential element of designing a product that works for customers as it is the function most likely to identify customers subject to harm, often due to notification from the customer themselves, and issue the required support to those customers. Equally the harm may be related to a change in the customer's circumstances which has resulted in them being unable to meet their financial objectives through the current product. A well-functioning customer support provision will enable flexibility within the product or for the customer to switch easily – thus addressing the customer's needs. Support functions, such as call centres, are expensive so it is a matter of good faith that firms have adequate provision to support their customers.

3.2: Product Governance Framework – Manufacturers

Probably the main aspect of the Duty for manufacturers is the product governance framework. This is consistent with other product governance frameworks already required by the regulator, such as those set out in the PROD section of the FCA Handbook, a set of standards applicable to MiFID investment firms, CRD firms, MiFID optional exemption firms, branches of third country investment firms (PROD 3), insurance firms (PROD 4), extended warranty providers (PROD 5), investment distribution (PROD 6) and funeral plan providers (PROD 7). The framework required by the Duty mostly replicates the PROD framework.

The subsequent chapters in this book set out the framework expected under the Duty, both from a manufacturer's point of view and that of a distributor. It should be noted that where a firm is subject to PROD 3, 4 or 7 and the product falls within the scope of PROD, the firm has the choice whether to apply the relevant PROD provision or the Duty.

3.3: Product Governance Framework – Distributors

> "Firms are distributors if they offer, sell, recommend, advise on, arrange, deal, propose, or provide a product or service, including at renewal" (FCA FG22/15).

On the one hand it is obvious that the product governance framework is simplified for distributors, because their primary role is to take instruction from the manufacturer and follow it. However, the complex nature of some distribution chains requires distributors to take more responsibility than they might have previously. Take wealth management for example, where the chain can consist of multiple manufacturers (such as the investments themselves and the wrappers), co-manufacturers, and several distributors (such as the platform itself, the broker, or the financial advisor). In such situations the distributor will, on a practical level, need a formal process which enables them to identify their role in the distribution of the product, obligations placed on them by the manufacturer or co-manufacturers, and the effect that their policies may have on customers.

The FCA, in their final guidance, confirm that distributors must have distribution arrangements for each product or service they distribute, and this must:

- avoid causing and, where that is not practical, mitigate foreseeable harm to customers
- support management of conflicts of interest
- ensure the needs, characteristics and objectives of the target market are taken into account

To achieve this the distributor must understand the products and services they distribute. This must be accomplished through obtaining enough suitable information from the manufacturer to properly understand the target market, their characteristics, the characteristics of the product or service, the intended distribution strategy and required provisions for vulnerable customers. The distributor must then design their strategy around the product and customer needs whilst ensuring they manage conflicts of interest.

Managing Conflicts of Interest

There are several conflicts which may arise during a distributor's work. Obvious examples include those arising from client relationships such as incentives for certain products, discretionary commission payments, or the option to place customers with a product which confers a further benefit to the distributor. The distributor must have a distribution strategy which identifies and manages such risks.

Equally conflicts could arise from the internal policy of the distributor. One example cited in the FCA's final guidance is commission payments to staff based on sales where such remuneration structures incentivise a staff member to place a customer with a product when another would better suit their needs. Taking this further, it follows that any incentive structure which encourages staff to undertake an action which is not in the best interests of the customer, but of the firm, would be considered to be a conflict of interest and therefore one which must be managed by the distribution strategy. Quality monitoring is perhaps the most common incentive structure which can have a significant impact on the behaviour of staff, often with unintended consequences. Generally, monitoring and other assurance work are not seen by firms as incentives, and thus not giving rise of to a conflict of interest. This approach is incorrect, especially where the results are channelled into performance reviews.

Therefore, a well-defined distribution strategy can include commission or bonus payments, however these should be designed around providing the customer with the best option for their needs rather than the most profitable option for the firm.

Data Sharing

Clearly the relationship between a manufacturer and distributor requires a significant level of information to be shared. As detailed above the distribution strategy created by a distributor must be centred around the intended benefits to the target market, characteristics of the target market, and the manufacturer's intended distribution strategy and/or instruction. This information is the minimum that needs to be shared between the manufacturer and distributor.

The Duty requires a continual review of each product, usually by way of product reviews and value assessments. The responsibility for the review rests on the manufacturer, however they may well be unable to accurately review the product or its value without certain key information from a distributor. Therefore, the FCA make it clear that distributors should support the manufacturer's reviews through sharing information when requested. This includes data in relation to sales, customer retention, customer feedback, complaints and changes the distributor has made to the strategy based on its own reviews. There is also a requirement for firms to notify relevant parties in the distribution chain if they identify consumer harm. If distributors identify information that should be shared with the manufacturer, they should provide it promptly. For example, where a distributor identifies foreseeable harm or problems with the way a product or service is operating in practice, then they should share that information as soon as possible. This level of co-operation applies to all firms in the distribution chain.

Proportionality

- The FCA state a distributor's governance framework must be proportionate to their role in the distribution chain. Where firms have little impact on the product the customer receives, or influence on which product the customer purchases, then a light touch approach may be used. Such an approach may be limited to assessing the manufacturer's instructions, ensuring adherence and meeting data reporting requirements. In the majority of cases this will already be captured as part of a distributor's contract / service level agreement adherence arrangements.

Equally there is a proportionality element to the data sharing expectations. In order to keep data requests manageable manufacturers can request samples of customer data, or organise focus groups, instead of requesting large volumes of raw data.

Products distributed on behalf of a non-UK manufacturer.

There is additional responsibility for distributors where they deliver a product which has been developed by a manufacturer outside of the scope of the Duty. The FCA state "A product or service may not have been approved in accordance with the obligations under the products and services outcome if it was developed by a firm outside the UK. In this case, distributors must comply with the obligations on distributors under the rules for this outcome. They must for example, take all reasonable steps to understand the product or service and the target market it would serve in order to ensure it will be distributed appropriately" (FCA FG22/5). It therefore follows that distributors will need to take steps to identify the target market, their characteristics, foreseeable harms and take steps to distribute the product appropriately.

Monitoring

As with any other aspect of FCA regulation, monitoring arrangements must be included in the product governance framework. This is in order to assess whether the framework is achieving its aims.

Distributors must regularly review whether:

- their distribution arrangements are appropriate and up to date

- products and services have been distributed to customers in the target market
- the product governance framework is functioning to comply with the cross-cutting rules.

An example is an Independent Financial Advisor distributing on behalf of several discretionary fund managers. Each fund will provide detailed information about their service, target market and suitability. These aspects, together with practical requirements, make up the distribution arrangements which must be followed by the IFA.

The IFA must also take steps to ensure the distribution arrangements are functioning as expected and are up to date. The obvious way is to liaise with the fund manager at regular intervals, at least on an annual basis, although certain events may also trigger the review including:

- identification by the IFA that the product may be unsuitable for groups of customers not excluded from purchasing the product
- the distribution strategy is not functioning as expected
- economic or other events changing the risk profile of the product
- lack of use of the product / aspects of the product or any other information the distributor becomes aware of which may indicate that the product is not appropriate for customers in the target market.

As indicated above, the distributor must also review whether the product has been distributed to customers in the stated target market. The IFA may, as part of their outcomes monitoring, conduct an analysis of customers, comparing them to those in the target market. Where the result is that the product has been wrongly distributed, an assessment of whether the distribution arrangements are appropriate and up to date will be triggered.

Finally, the IFA should assess, at least annually, whether their product governance framework is facilitating compliance with the cross-cutting rules. The assessment can be conducted through analysis of the outcomes received by customers where those who have been unable to achieve their stated objectives are identified as well as customers who have clearly received harm. This can be supported by specific 'good faith' audits looking at the IFA's financial promotions, other materials, and procedures to identify instances where profit may have been prioritised over customer outcomes. Again, the result, if negative, would trigger a further assessment of the appropriateness of the distribution strategy alongside the manufacturer.

3.4: Relationship with the Cross-cutting rules

As manufacturers work through the product governance framework, the cross-cutting rules must be applied throughout. The product approval process is the starting point in the governance framework with the FCA stating "A manufacturer must maintain, operate and review a process for the approval of: (1) a product, and (2) significant adaptations to a product" (PRIN 2A.3.2R) and "a manufacturer's product approval procedures must:

1. specify the target market for the product at a sufficiently granular level, taking into account the characteristics, risk profile, complexity and nature of the product;

2. take account of any particular additional or different needs, characteristics and objectives that might be relevant for retail customers in the target market with characteristics of vulnerability;

3. ensure that all relevant risks to the target market, including any relevant risks to retail customers with characteristics of vulnerability, are assessed;

4. ensure that the design of the product:

    a. meets the needs, characteristics and objectives of the target market.

    b. does not adversely affect groups of retail customers in the target market, including groups of retail customers with characteristics of vulnerability; and

    c. avoids causing foreseeable harm in the target market;

5. ensure that the intended distribution strategy is appropriate for the target market; and

6. require the manufacturer to take all reasonable steps to ensure that the product is distributed to the identified target market."

(PRIN 2A.3.4R)

As a manufacturer conducts the approval process, they will identify the target market and characteristics of customers in that target market, and then use this information to identify where there is a risk of non-compliance with the cross-cutting rules. The cross-cutting rules are outlined in more detail in the next chapter, for now a high-level summary will suffice.

The cross-cutting rules require firms to:

1. Act in good faith toward retail customers. This can be summarised by the requirement for organisations to put the customer's needs at the centre of their operations and business models, at least on a par with profitability.

2. Avoid causing foreseeable harm to retail customers. Every financial product will be associated with some inherent risk. The Duty does not require such 'naturally occurring' risk to be removed, instead avoiding causing foreseeable harm means taking steps to identify and avoid the harms which could occur from the organisation's business practices. Whilst it is also expected that organisations do what they can to limit the risk of inherent and other harms in their products, it is not a requirement to remove the risk of harm altogether. Instead, remedy can be achieved through ensuring the customer is given information in relation to the potential harm in a manner which enables them to make effective decisions.

3. Enable and support retail customers to pursue their financial objectives. For the majority of firms this simply involves ensuring that customers can 'use and enjoy' the full expected benefits of the product or service. This definition specifically works for firms acting on a non-advised basis where they won't become aware of the customer's wider financial objectives or situation. Conversely, where an advice service is provided, a greater focus should be placed on compliance with this rule as it is the manufacturer's responsibility to understand the customer's objectives and take steps to meet them.

The link between the cross-cutting rules and product approvals is best illustrated through an example. Take an insurance provider who intends to bring a life insurance product to the market. Under the Duty they must complete the product approval process. In doing so they will identify the nature of the product, its intended benefit(s), the target market and their characteristics. For example, the life insurance provider may have identified those under 30 years old as underserved by life insurance products and therefore aim the product towards this group of customers. As such they design the product so the rate at which the payment on death falls is slower than others on the market, and the monthly payment amount is adjusted depending on the person's age. There will be other steps the manufacturer will take to design the product for the target market but for this example we will focus on these features.

The manufacturer then must analyse the intended target market in order to identify their characteristics. We will focus on the defining feature of this product: age. The manufacturer undertakes market research and utilises established industry research to identify that those under 30 generally have less experience with financial services, particularly services for which the benefit would not be realised for a significant period of time, such as life insurance. They also identify they are more likely to buy on impulse, failing to think about the long term. From a financial perspective under 30s have lower levels of secured debt, such as mortgages but a higher debt to income ratio of unsecured debt. Furthermore, they typically earn less and have lower job security.

Now that the manufacturer understands the target market's characteristics, they can identify the harms which may occur. Resulting from the lack of financial experience, one harm is that they may not understand the product, whether they need it, or even what it is for. Appreciating this need allows the manufacturer to adjust the information provided when marketing the product, on-boarding the customer, and even post-sale to provide those explanations. Building a pause into the on-boarding process, where suitability is assessed, would be a useful step to avoid foreseeable harm. This would allow the customer's circumstances to be reviewed, identifying whether they need the product, would benefit from it, and offering the opportunity to assess whether they understand it. In this scenario we have assumed a sale on an advised basis, whereas we might expect the manufacturer to want to bring the product to market through a range of distribution channels, online for example. The manufacturer should consider how they can replicate the information and advice through all channels.

Taking the steps outlined in the above paragraph also demonstrates good faith through balancing financial promotions to include information about the risks of the product, such as any limitations or exclusions, to placing friction in the sales journey, enabling potential customers to pause and consider whether the product is right for them. Additionally, this friction helps to reduce the risk of impulse buying, an identified characteristic of the under 30s market.

The analysis of the target market also focused on the financial stability of typical under 30s. With increased risk of job loss and generally lower earning potential, the manufacturer may well decide to build flexibility into the product, such as a period of time whereby payments can be paused, should the customer fall into financial difficulty in order to support the customer's financial objectives. Utilising the payment break may only have a small impact on the value of any payout, it would be fair for the manufacturer to design the product in this way. It would not be fair to design it to prevent any claim being made during the break period, or to cancel the policy altogether. Such deep thought about the product and what is, and is not, fair is exactly what the Duty is aiming to achieve. Traditionally some insurers may have targeted such situations to cancel policies, for obvious reasons of profitability, or may have targeted customer markets less likely to be able to keep up with payments. The Duty is designed to prevent products being designed in this way.

Outcomes Monitoring

Product governance does not stop at the approval process, the outcomes received by customers must be measured throughout the product journey. PRIN 2A.9 places an obligation on firms to monitor the outcomes their customers are receiving from their products. As with product approvals, testing of customer outcomes must be against the cross-cutting rules, with PRIN 2A.9.2G confirming "The purpose of the monitoring obligation is to enable firms to identify whether there are any risks that they are not meeting the requirements of the cross-cutting obligations and the retail customer outcomes, and consequently they are not acting to deliver good outcomes for retail customers."

Monitoring can best be seen as a series of measures set against key risk indicators. The manufacturer and/or distributor should undertake a process to identify applicable KRIs to each of their products, or where it is impossible to do so, perhaps due to the number of products offered by the organisation, through using a risk-based approach. Broadly, there are three techniques which can be used to identify the risks.

The first is to derive the risks from the product approval. If the process has been completed thoroughly and in according with PRIN requirements there should be a rich set of risks already identified and likely classified by each of the cross-cutting rules with foreseeable harms providing the majority of KRIs to be measured.

The second is to complete a simple review of the product type, identifying the risks typically associated with the product. There are obvious risks, such as credit default, mortgage arrears, investment loss and inappropriate / disproportionate insurance cover. However more thought is needed to locate all significant issues which could indicate poor customer outcomes. Organisations may look at whether all of the product's features are being used, particularly where there has been a charge levied for the inclusion of that product feature. How customers react to communications, particularly those which are designed to provoke a response from a customer to take steps which support good outcomes may also be included in reviews.

Thirdly, is to use historic data to identify where customer outcomes have not been positive. Reviews should analyse data such as default, arrears, switching and cancellation data as well as complaints and poor outcomes identified from quality monitoring. However, this final option does rely on the availability of data and extensive work to focus the work of monitoring teams on customer outcomes, so they are able to consistently identify poor outcomes.

Fair Value

It is important to note that the FCA has a real focus on fair value. Constant citing of the outcome as well as regulatory intervention in the first year of the Duty appears to demonstrate value will be front and centre of the FCA's priority list. The product governance framework must be equally as focused on fair value, with the measure of value weighted against the cross-cutting rules. This can be achieved through inclusion of detailed value assessments during product approvals which are revisited as outcomes are monitored.

Monitoring outcomes in relation to fair value is a sizable task because there are multiple factors to consider, including the price paid (both monetary and non-monetary), service received by the customer, and market factors which could result in the product failing to provide value. At a minimum firms should review:

1. whether the customer is getting what they have paid for, if the product was sold with the expectation of certain features, have those features been provided?

2. If additional charges (for example, discretionary charges such as late payment fees) represent the true cost to the business.

3. Where the product is linked to an external measure which impacts the cost to the customer or return to the customer in the case of savings accounts or investments, whether there has been a significant change resulting in a lack of value. Such a lack of value will be present where other products on the market become better value for the customer.

4. Whether vulnerable customers are paying more for the same service or paying the same and not using all of the benefits.

5. Whether customers' behavioural biases impact the value received by some customers.

6. Whether customers who have accessed the product through different distribution channels receive different outcomes including cost or product usage.

7. When considering value, charges that may be applied or accrued throughout the life of the product must be considered.

The cross-cutting rules apply in tandem with the areas listed above. Organisations are looking for foreseeable harms which derive from a lack of value, such as a customer not receiving all or part of the service they have paid for. It is, however, the financial objective cross-cutting rule which interacts with fair value the most as the two are intrinsically linked. If a customer's financial objective is to open a savings account and achieve the best rate possible for their circumstances, should the market significantly change over the course of the agreement, the manufacturer will need to identify the product is no longer meeting the customer's financial objectives.

Ultimately it is a matter of good faith to pro-actively seek out instances where a business is making too much profit from a customer and take steps to rebalance the relationship. Manufacturers are bound to do so, however, due to the cross-cutting rules.

CHAPTER FOUR

CROSS-CUTTING RULES

4.1: Good Faith

The cross-cutting rules should not be seen as stand-alone requirements, instead they are to be applied alongside the four outcomes. The first, acting in good faith, underpins all actions taken by manufacturers and distributors. It must be demonstrated in all that firms do.

The rule

PRIN 2A.2.2 states "Acting in good faith is a standard of conduct characterised by honesty, fair and open dealing and acting consistently with the reasonable expectations of retail customers." Guidance is provided in PRIN 2A.2.3 in the form of examples of not acting in good faith. These can be summarised as exploiting customers, manipulating customers to their detriment, carrying out an action more quickly or to a higher standard when it benefits the firm compared to when it only benefits the customer, and exploiting a customer's behavioural bias.

It is clear this rule has been developed due to practices the regulator has seen since its creation in 2013 as well as historic scandals where similar behaviours were evident. They include financial services firms designing products and services to the sole benefit of the firm, regardless of the impact on customers. Applying this lens when designing products results in issues such as unbalanced financial promotions, unclear charging structures, price walking and reduced access to support.

Defining 'good faith'

In FG 22/5 good faith is described as the act of being open and honest to support the weaker bargaining position that most customers find themselves in, therefore the starting point is to recognise the imbalance of power between firm and customer. Inequal knowledge and capability is the most common source of imbalance, it is important to take account of this when designing the product and take steps to support customers where appropriate. Others include time and resource, sales practices which use time investment strategies to gain a sale would therefore fall foul of these rules. Such strategies include holding back elements of the cost until after the customer has invested their time and effort inputting details or completing checks, making it more likely they will accept the charges.

The FCA's guidance goes on to explain good faith as the intent behind actions and a firm would not be acting in good faith if they failed to take the circumstances of customers into account. Specific examples include the way in which firms may present information, such as designing its flow and prominence to take advantage of the customer's behavioural biases or lack of understanding. One example cited is a financial promotion where the potential benefits of the product are overvalued compared to the risks. Another is giving more weight to immediate benefits compared to effects that are further away, such as positioning monthly earnings front and centre of the promotion whilst only mentioning termination charges in the small print. The need for balance does not stop with financial promotions, it is clear this requirement applies throughout the entire customer journey as similar techniques can be used to encourage certain contact methods, discourage product switching/cancelation, or take up at renewal.

Culture

The FCA's final guidance explains "Firms also need to ensure that their culture supports and is conducive to their staff acting in good faith. A firm is unlikely to be able to act in good faith if it uses staff incentives, performance management or remuneration structures which are likely to cause detriment to their customers". (FG 22/5, page 30). For the proper implementation of the Duty this is an important concept to understand. It requires a deep cultural change in many businesses and this is the very core of what the Duty is trying to achieve. To understand it we first must look at how firms measured their performance prior to the Duty and for many the ultimate, sometimes only, measure of success was profit. Whilst the Duty is not aimed at disregarding profit altogether it recognises that measuring only by profit only is flawed. This is because, despite a strong bottom line, a number of factors could be occurring at the same time. Perhaps the organisation is generating high levels of sales through mis-selling, leaving their customer base dissatisfied which, in turn, chips away at the firm's reputation. Eventually this could catch-up with the firm, reducing sales in the long term. In a culture where success is measured by profit only, this type of risk can easily go un-noticed. A similar set of risks, driven by the same culture, were allowed to fester in the early 2000s, leading to the credit crunch. In this example we have focused on the effect on profitability, allowing customer dissatisfaction to go un-noticed can lead to multiple other negative outcomes: reduced customer retention, higher levels of complaints and increased redress repayments to name a few. The biggest risk, as has been seen several times over the last decade, arises from claims management. If the product falls into the awareness of such firms, and they identify wide-spread practice, a deluge of claims, complaints and therefore redress can come the way of the manufacturer. Firms simply cannot afford to fail to measure their performance by customer outcomes.

To combat the potential issues identified in the preceding paragraph, the requirement to ensure a culture that supports and is conducive to their staff acting in good faith can only be achieved by measuring business success against wider metrics than profit alone: targets based around customer satisfaction and product / service success should be developed. To create these, the management of an organisation needs to be able to view the company's offerings through the eyes of their customers – a consumer lens. When the products are viewed through the eyes of the customer, organisations are able to develop a number of quality-based targets which, if applied, have the potential to completely change the way in which a team see a firm's goals, the purpose of the service, and their own functions. Take financial promotions as an example, for as long as can be remembered those developing marketing material have been measured against the number of sales their advert delivered. Clearly, this measurement does not encourage marketing departments to create balanced, good faith promotions. Instead, it encourages them to play-down potential risks and draw customers in through playing up the potential benefits. They are not concerned with whether the product the right for the customer or with the outcome customers receive. Now, imagine the marketing team is measured by whether the advert succeeded in attracting the intended target market. This completely changes the motivations of the creator, instead incentivising them to provide customers with the right information to make an informed choice.

<u>Redress</u>

Good faith also involves providing redress where it is due and being pro-active about it. In early 2024 the FCA wrote to a number of wealth management firms with three questions:

1. How many customers have paid to receive an annual review?

2. How many customers have received the annual review?

3. Have you refunded customers who have paid but not received the review?

This example highlights the proactivity the regulator is expecting firms to meet the good faith threshold. Before the Duty, it was unlikely that many firms would think to offer refunds to customers where they don't use all or part of a service, however the questions posed by the FCA do indicate that this is now the expected norm.

Ultimately acting in good faith comes down to the need to avoid designing products and services through the sole lens of business profitability. Taking appropriate measures to protect customers and avoid actively designing the service to enable higher charges to be levied without added value for the customer is now required for compliance with the Duty.

Distributors

The good faith requirement clearly impacts manufacturers, but it also applies to distributors. Distributors will play a lesser role in the design of the product, but they do need to demonstrate good faith whilst undertaking their activities associated with the product. Distributors should review the distribution arrangements supplied by manufacturers prior to use and support manufacturers to identify any risks that they may not have identified. Furthermore, distributors should also apply the same arrangements as manufacturers to the governance of their organisations, taking the steps we have described in relation to performance measures to change the culture, from one of profit first, to a customer centric operation.

4.2: Foreseeable Harm

The Rule

Front and centre of the cross-cutting rules is foreseeable harm. PRIN 2A.2.8 sets out the high-level requirement to avoid foreseeable harms with PRIN 2A.2.9 clarifying that harms may be caused by act or omission including where the harm is actually contributed to by another firm in the distribution chain.

This cross-cutting rule requires the most attention due to its position within the product governance framework. This position is highlighted by PRIN 2A.2.10 which lists ways in which firms can avoid foreseeable harm. The first requires the manufacturer to ensure "all aspects of the design, terms, marketing, sale of and support for its products avoid causing foreseeable harm" (PRIN 2A.2.10G) as well as "taking appropriate action to mitigate the risk of actual or foreseeable harm, including for example by: (i) updating or otherwise amending the design of the product or distribution strategy; (ii) updating information about a product or updating investment advice; (iii) ensuring that retail customers do not face unreasonable barriers (including unreasonable additional costs), for example when they want to switch products or providers or to complain; (iv) allowing time and support for retail customers to find suitable alternatives where a product is withdrawn."

When

Foreseeable harms are therefore the key consideration for manufacturers when they complete the product approval process. As manufacturers identify the nature of the service on offer, the cross-cutting rules require them to identify the harms which could naturally occur due to that service and take steps to avoid or mitigate such harms, where possible. Investment loss, home repossession, default and arrears are all such harms.

The approval process then moves onto the target market and their characteristics, again presenting an opportunity for the manufacturer to identify and remove foreseeable harms, this time linked with the characteristics of the expected target market. Examples include poor understanding of financial products, lack of financial ability to absorb loss, poor IT skills as well as certain vulnerabilities.

Once the product has been launched it becomes the role of outcomes monitoring, product reviews and value assessments to identify harms occurring, taking steps to mitigate or remove those harms.

How

The product governance requirements ask the manufacturer to take steps to ensure the distribution strategy is appropriate, as per PRIN 2A.2.10 this means designing it to avoid or mitigate the risk of foreseeable harm. The FCA included a useful example in the final guidance. The example was one of a wealth management firm who had designed a high-risk investment option. Recognising the high-risk nature of the product they carefully define the target market to include those who are able to absorb the loss and have the relevant risk appetite. To help ensure the correct target market is reached they design a distribution strategy which involves only selling the product with advice and selecting distributors able to offer this advice.

The definition of 'distribution strategy' should be read widely, it is more than the initial distribution to customers, i.e. sales; it includes all elements of customer interaction and service, both pre and post-sale as confirmed by PRIN 2A.2.11: "A firm with an ongoing relationship with a retail customer in relation to a product would need to act to avoid causing foreseeable harm to that customer throughout the lifecycle of that product." As such the mitigating actions stemming from the identification of harms may stretch into post-sale activity, such as customer support provision. To highlight this point, we will borrow the FCA's example of the high-risk investment product. In this scenario the manufacturer identified that the product is only suitable to individuals with a high-risk appetite and ability to absorb losses. Every effort was made to reach this target market during the sale, but the manufacturer should recognise that a customer's circumstances might change during the investment period, as such they may build a specific question into their annual review looking at this point and provide training to support staff as to what to do should a customer's circumstances change.

Another example is allowing customers to cancel or switch where appropriate, building in routes to do so which are not overly onerous (this is also required as part of acting in good faith). In the investment example we talked about an annual review and whilst this is an important step, the customer requires a solution to be provided after the review. Switching to another product, either with the same firm or another, could well be the solution a customer, whose circumstances have changed, needs. Alternatively, it may be the case that it is now in their best interests to cancel the product altogether.

PRIN 2A.2.10G requires firms to offer both time and support to enable customers to find alternatives in the case that a product is withdrawn.

Limitations

This cross-cutting rule only requires firms to avoid harms which are reasonably foreseeable, therefore the question of 'what is foreseeable' is then raised. The final guidance offers the following: "Whether harm is considered foreseeable would depend on whether a prudent firm acting reasonably would be able to predict or expect the ultimately harmful result of their action or omission in connection with the product or service" (FG 22/5 page 31) and "As the Duty is underpinned by the concept of reasonableness, firms are only responsible for addressing the risk of harm when it is reasonably foreseeable at the time, considering what a firm knows, or could reasonably be expected to have known. This will depend in part on the information the firm collects as part of its business, and this in turn will depend on the scale, service offering and capabilities of the firm. However, we expect all firms to collect enough information to be able to act to avoid causing foreseeable harm" (FG 22/5, page 32).

An important consideration is in relation to distribution chains. Often the harm won't be caused by the manufacturer but by another in the chain, therefore understanding the regulator's expectations is paramount to understanding where responsibilities sit. For example, SYSC 8 is quite clear that the responsibility for good customer outcomes and compliance rests both with the firm outsourcing and with the supplier, where the supplier is undertaking regulated activity. Whilst the FCA has been careful not to place equivalent expectations on manufacturers, stating they are not responsible for the compliance of distributors with the Duty, there are several aspects which do establish joint liability. PRIN 2A.2.9 is one of those aspects, where it places an obligation on firms to look at the whole distribution chain to ascertain where foreseeable harms may occur and take active steps to avoid them. The same section of PRIN highlights that harms may be caused by omission. It therefore follows that firms identifying harms to customers, due to the actions of another firm in the distribution chain, should take steps to avoid the harm occurring.

Distributors

This chapter has focused on the steps a manufacturer should take to avoid foreseeable harm, it is just as important to consider the role of distributors as the cross-cutting rules apply to both manufacturers and distributors. Distributors are required to take steps to avoid foreseeable harm through:

(i) Familiarising themselves with the manufacturer's instructions, specifically any distribution arrangements.

(ii) Following the instructions provided by manufacturers.

(iii) Understanding the intended target market and their characteristics, highlighting to the manufacturer where the product is not reaching the intended market.

(iv) Being aware of harms which could be caused by the product or the characteristics of customers, identify when these are occurring and take steps to avoid harm as well as alerting the manufacturer.

(v) To provide information to the manufacturer to enable them to conduct reviews, outcomes monitoring and identify harms occurring .

Whilst it is incumbent on the manufacturer to design the product and distribution strategy to avoid harms where possible, there is nothing preventing the distributor from undertaking their own review and pro-active steps to avoid harms, although the extent to which the distributor needs to take steps will depend on its role and extent of influence over customer outcomes (FG 22/5, page 31).

For both manufacturers and distributors, it is worth noting that this cross-cutting rule does not create a fiduciary Duty, nor does it require that all harm is avoided, this is often impossible. The guidance in PRIN 2A.2.13G explains that the inherent risks within a product do not need to be avoided, instead the focus should be on ensuring the customer understands and accepts those risks.

Oversight

Avoiding foreseeable harms is likely to consume much of the thinking and resources allocated for the Duty. For this reason, the consumer Duty champion may wish to pay particular attention to the steps their organisations have taken to identify and avoid harms. The primary roles of the consumer Duty champion are to promote the Duty throughout the different levels within the organisation and provide challenge to actions taken. There are a number of points the champion can look at, guided by the FCA's final guidance, in order to challenge a firm's approach to comply with this rule, including:

- Whether the firm has proactively considered how consumers' behavioural biases, such as inertia, might lead their products or services to cause foreseeable harm.

- Have the products or services changed and if so has there been an assessment of new harms which could arise?

- Can any new or emerging harms be identified through MI, complaints, external risks or from the FCA's supervisory work?

- Are processes enabling customers to cancel a service, or switch provider easy for customers to understand and use?

- Are customers incurring higher charges than needed due to a lack of understanding of the product?
- Is there evidence of vulnerable customers being unable to use or access a product or part of the associated service?
- Are customers falling victim to financial crimes, such as scams, due to inadequate procedures to prevent and detect such crime?

4.3: Financial Objectives

The rule

Firms must act to enable and support customers to pursue their financial objectives.

A consumer's financial objective is normally defined by their purchase of a product and service with PRIN 2A.2.16G explaining that a firm providing an execution only service can assume the customer's objective is to "use and enjoy the full benefits of the product in question" (PRIN 2A.2.16G). Whereas for advised sales the firm must take steps to understand more about the objectives of the customer and advise accordingly.

There are, however, some limitations. For example, situations where the customer did not disclose their full circumstances, perhaps missing information which is vital in order to provide advice aimed at achieving their objectives. In such circumstances the firm is largely protected by PRIN 2A.2.17G which says, "A firm which provides advisory or discretionary services is entitled to rely on the objectives that retail customers have disclosed unless it knows or could reasonably be expected to know that information disclosed is manifestly out of date, inaccurate or incomplete."

Nevertheless, the FCA is trying to strike a balance between the customer's own responsibilities and a firm's obligation to protect the interests of customers. Information is the key to achieving this balance; with the clear expectation that manufacturers and distributors take reasonable steps to gather the information they need to understand the customer's financial objectives and meet these (advised service) or the information required to assess whether the product is suitable for the customer and therefore likely to meet their needs (both advised and non-advised services). Simply asking the relevant questions, however, will not be enough on its own. The barometer of reasonable steps includes factoring the customer's behavioural biases and vulnerability into the likelihood of the customer providing the required information.

It is important to consider the methods used to request the information. To meet the Duty standard, information gathering must be conducted in a manner in which it is likely that a customer, with the characteristics typically found in the target market, would provide the information. Firms must show they have taken every measure possible to gather information from customers and provided customers with the information they need, in a way which is understandable for customers in the target market, and at the right time to enable them to make informed decisions in relation to their financial objectives. This comes back to the product governance framework and the steps an organisation has taken to properly understand their target market.

Information needs

The FCA's final guidance sets out the regulator's expectations in relation to communication and supporting financial objectives. Firms should comply through:

- considering the characteristics of the customers that their communications are aimed at and tailoring their communications accordingly so that they are likely to be understood

- helping customers navigate the information the firm provides, making it easy for consumers to identify the key information and their available options, and

- having systems and processes in place to test and monitor the impact of communications on consumer understanding and using the outputs to improve their communications

  (FG 22/5, page 36)

Therefore, a vital component of supporting customers to pursue their financial objectives is to provide the right information, at the right time, in the right way to enable customers to make informed decisions.

Consumer support

The type of support that customers need depends upon the type of service provided and of course, the characteristics of the target market. Manufacturers are obliged to consider the support customers may require to help them to follow their financial goals. Beyond information needs this may also include the availability of well-trained staff to answer questions and assist customers to take actions on their accounts, in cases where the target market has additional support needs those staff members will need to be specifically trained to be able to provide the level of support required by the customer.

At a minimum, customers with disabilities must be supported to be able to access both the product and post-sale support, often taking the form of revised communications, such as providing correspondence in braille, throughout the customers' journey. To fully comply with the spirit of this rule such reasonable adjustments should also be provided to all customers with additional support needs, including vulnerable customers, those who may find it difficult to understand complex communication, or customers who may find it difficult to access or use part of a service such as those with a lack of financial experience.

Further to the above, the final guidance provides three examples that firms can take to support a customer to pursue their financial objectives, all three examples focus on the design of the customer support provision:

"Through consumer support (see Chapter 9) firms can support customers in pursuing their financial objectives by:

- designing and delivering consumer support in a way that does not create unreasonable barriers to consumers realising the benefits of products and services or acting in their interests

- ensuring that their consumer support enables consumers to fully use the products and services they buy and supports them in acting in their own interests: this includes avoiding 'sludge' in the design of consumer journeys, which uses friction to prevent consumers from taking actions such as cancelling a product or amending terms

- ensuring that the channels of support they provide work effectively and do not act as a barrier to customers utilising their products, cancelling or switching to another provider should they wish to".

(FG22/5, page 37)

The Duty does stop short at requiring firms to provide information to customers about cheaper options with other providers or provide a cheaper product itself. Instead, the focus is on enabling the customer to switch, or move product, should they ask to do so. Furthermore, organisations are not required to go beyond the scope of their regulatory permissions and provide advice where this is not part of the services of the firm.

When

As with the other cross-cutting rules, financial objectives must be met at all stages of the customer journey. In order to achieve this, the support likely to be required by customers should be identified at the product design stage (or product review stage for products which pre-date the consumer Duty) and built into the distribution strategy.

The information needs of customers must also be considered at the product design stage as do the information needs of the firm, to enable appropriate advice to be provided or to enable an informed decision about the product to be made. This must then be reviewed on an ongoing basis, to ascertain whether the design of the product has been successful in meeting these needs. The firm's outcomes monitoring, value assessments and product reviews will provide the framework for the assessments to be made.

Value assessments play an important role, as a firm can only enable a customer to pursue their financial objectives if the product or service offered is of fair value, therefore a point in time during which this rule must be considered is when a firm conducts the assessment of value. This extends beyond the core product charges to conditional fees, especially any fee charged for exiting the product as such a fee can clearly impact a customer's financial choices.

As a result, it is safe to say the FCA requires manufacturers and distributors to be able to use two lenses when applying this rule. The first is via a product based view, when designing products and services, ensuring they are designed to meet the information needs of customers in the target market. The second is on an individual basis, when interacting with customers, this is more likely to be implemented through guidance and training for front line staff.

Declining a customer

One result of the requirement to enable and support customers to achieve their financial objective is likely to be an increase in firms declining customers. This is because firms are starting to understand their customers better, their goals and circumstances in particular, and so it follows that, often, the correct advice would be to not purchase the product. It is important to note that the firm still have a Duty to the customer, even in this situation. As such they can support a customer to achieve their objectives through providing information. This information could be designed to guide the customer to make good choices or sign-post customers to reliable advice, such as free debt advice or the Citizens Advice Bureau.

Distributors

As highlighted earlier, whilst the product design is the responsibility of manufacturers, often the delivery of all or part of the product may well be the responsibility of the distributor. In these cases, the role of the distributor is clear, to understand and follow the manufacturer's instructions and follow those instructions. On the face of it, this appears to be a simple requirement, however, in practice, it may well be difficult to implement successfully. The overarching difficulty is the very nature of having an organisation, separate to your own, setting requirements you must follow and the fact that your company may not be in a position to satisfy their instructions in the manner expected. The manufacturer may require certain, specialist, advice or information to be provided alongside the sale, which the distributor may not be set up to provide.

There also may well be several methods of achieving the same aim, for example the manufacturer may have identified the need to undertake stringent creditworthiness assessments to help customers achieve their financial objectives but decide to implement this through requiring manufacturers to use the Standard Financial Statement. However, the distributor's systems may be set up to use a different style of creditworthiness assessment which is equally as robust.

Furthermore, a distributor working on behalf of several manufacturers are faced with the challenge of meeting multiple similar, often competing requirements. This example can be highlighted by a debt collection agency working on behalf of several creditors, each with their own distinct target market and opinions on how best to meet the financial objectives of their customers. In practice, with system limitations and cost management, it can be problematic to work to several standards at the same time. This especially can impact front line agents who may have to adapt to different standards for each call they make.

4.4: Summary

The relationship between the cross-cutting rules and the outcomes are best described by the FCA in FG 22/5, where they state "the cross-cutting rules also inform and are supported by the four outcomes which set out more detailed rules in key areas of the customer relationship, including the following points, for example:

- "Firms acting in good faith in their interactions and communications with customers is an essential element of complying with the outcome rules on consumer understanding and consumer support.
- Firms should act to avoid causing foreseeable harm in the way that they design and price products and services and make this a key objective of how they comply with the relevant outcome rules.
- Providing effective communications that customers can understand, and effective consumer support are an essential way in which firms act to enable and support customers to pursue their financial objectives, by creating the right environment for this.

- The cross-cutting rules also help firms interpret the four outcomes. For example, one way for a firm to know a product does not offer fair value, would be if it were to lead to foreseeable harm.

- The cross-cutting rules also help define the overarching standards of conduct firms should follow in areas not explicitly dealt with through the four outcomes, so compliance with the four outcomes would not be exhaustive of what the Principle or cross-cutting rules require"

  FG22/5: Final non-Handbook Guidance for firms on the Consumer Duty (fca.org.uk)

CHAPTER FIVE

PRODUCT APPROVALS: MANUFACTURERS

5.1: Assessment Trigger

Trigger

PRIN 2A.3 is the starting point of the framework, requiring manufacturers to "maintain, operate and review a process of approval" (FCA Handbook: PRIN 2A.3.2R) in relation to a new product or upon significantly adapting a product. The same section requires the process to occur before the product is marketed or distributed to retail customers. The definition of retail customers shares the meaning of 'retail market business' as outlined in chapter one of this book.

However, the definition of the term 'product' needs to be examined as it is wider than it would appear on the face of it. A product is a 'specified investment', payment service or e-money issuance (the definition of specified investment is extremely wide, essentially encompassing any regulated activity) which involves or includes regulated activity or ancillary activity where the service is provided to a retail customer (either directly or not). The addition of 'ancillary activity' brings a range of activities into the scope of the product definition, for example a debt collection agency designing a collections process will need to be aware that the collection process is a classified as a product and therefore need to conduct a product approval. Additionally, they could, depending on the level of autonomy given to them by the creditor, be a manufacturer.

It does not matter whether the product has previously been distributed, meaning this provision applies to products already 'live' before 31 July 2023 (the Duty's implementation date).

Significantly Adapting a Product

The requirement applies to both new products and where a firm significantly adapts a product. As a result, it is important to explore the meaning of the word 'significantly' in this context. The finalised guidance (FG 22/5) has some helpful pointers, namely:

1. Where terms and conditions of the product remain the same, despite the fact that a customer may be investing into a different financial instrument or entering into a different mortgage contract

2. When considering number 1, one issue to consider is any fees or charges, if they remain the same it is unlikely that a product approval would be required

3. It is unlikely for the product to be considered significantly adapted where the terms and conditions have been amended to solely to add clarity.

It is likely the product would be considered to be new or significantly adapted:

4. Where the scope of the product changes, such as the level of insurance cover offered

5. Where a firm changes the features of a product in a way which impacts customers or changes the target market, or

6. Changes in the target market for other reasons.

5.2: Content of Assessment

For open products PRIN 2A.3.3 lists the required content of the approval as:

(1) specify the *target market* for the *product* at a sufficiently granular level, taking into account the characteristics, risk profile, complexity and nature of the *product*;

(2) take account of any particular additional or different needs, characteristics and objectives that might be relevant for *retail customers* in the *target market* with characteristics of vulnerability;

(3) ensure that all relevant risks to the *target market*, including any relevant risks to *retail customers* with characteristics of vulnerability, are assessed.

(4) ensure that the design of the *product*:

  (i) meets the needs, characteristics and objectives of the *target market*;

  (ii) does not adversely affect groups of *retail customers* in the *target market*, including groups of *retail customers* with characteristics of vulnerability; and

  (iii) avoids causing foreseeable harm in the *target market*;

(5) ensure that the intended distribution strategy is appropriate for the *target market*; and

(6) require the *manufacturer* to take all reasonable steps to ensure that the *product* is *distributed* to the identified *target market*.

(PRIN 2A.3 Consumer Duty: retail customer outcome – products and services – FCA Handbook)

The FCA, here, are inferring a logical flow to approvals beginning with an overview of the product (specifically why/how the product will benefit customers), followed by a description of the target market (i.e. those customers who would be in a position to realise the benefits of the product) and their characteristics (as defined below).

The purpose of understanding the customers' characteristics, as well as their objectives and needs, is to identify harm that could be caused to individuals with such characteristics, taking into account the nature of the product. The product and associated service can then be designed to minimise the likelihood of the identified harm occurring, or reducing its impact should it materialise. Moreover, firms are obliged to design the service provision, such as distribution strategy, customer communications and support options around the needs of the customers, therefore understanding their characteristics is an important first step.

Defining customer characteristics

FG 22/5 provides us with valuable insight as to the typical characteristics a manufacturer might identify as well as the required level of detail. The types of characteristics which may be identified include:

- age
- financial life stage
- financial experience
- education level
- reading age
- wealth / income
- attitude to risk

- vulnerabilities prevalent in the target market
- any other characteristic central to the design of your product

Vulnerability is important, not only because it is mentioned multiple times throughout the Duty, but because vulnerabilities prevalent in the target market must be considered using the following three stage process:

1. does/can the vulnerability type negatively impact the customer's access to, use, or enjoyment of the product?
2. does the above change depending on the severity of the vulnerability at any given time?
3. how can the product or service be designed to limit negative effects of the customers vulnerability?

Firms must also be mindful of the Equality Act 2010 when answering the above, ensuring that access to the product is not blocked due to a protected characteristic.

Example

A credit provider intends to introduce a new credit card, aimed at helping customers with poor credit history to rebuild their credit score. They need to complete a product approval. This details the inherent characteristics of the product including a credit check and creditworthiness assessment (in this case the assessment is lenient, enabling customers who would usually be deemed uncreditworthy access to the product). The company then undertakes research to properly understand the traits of customers likely to apply, including market research. This identifies that the product is most likely to be accessed by customers with lower financial understanding, low resilience, and low capability as well as customers with lower levels of education. As a result, the lender is able to identify foreseeable harms which could be caused to customers with these characteristics, including:

1. a lack of understanding of the credit product, specifically the difference between paying the balance in full each month and making minimum payments

2. failing to understand the risks and consequences of late payments

3. poor financial management skills potentially leading to missed payments

4. an average lower reading age making it difficult for some customers to understand complex correspondence.

They also identify a higher rate of vulnerability in the target market.

It is identified that these characteristics leave customers in the target market at a greater chance of entering into a credit product they don't fully understand, finding it difficult to navigate payment options, failing to understand the support that can be provided and with a higher chance of missing payments.

Therefore, the following solutions can be offered in order to mitigate the identified harms:

- Financial promotions designed to highlight the key risks of the product, not only the perceived benefits, and written in simple language within the typical reading capability of a 7–11-year-old.

- Friction is included in the sales journey to give the customer time to consider whether the product is right for them. At this point the nature of the product is clearly explained including the need for regular payments.

- The difference between making minimum payments and full payments each month is clearly explained as part of the sales journey, and the customer's affordability assessment is designed around full payments.

- The company puts in place additional support to guide customers regarding their financial management. This is designed as a 'support package' which customers can agree to during the purchase of the product or any time thereafter. There is no additional cost for this advice package.

- Customers receive regular payment reminders, before payments become overdue.

- Correspondence, including notifications of missed payments, are designed with the customer's average reading age and understanding of finance in mind.

The above is a simple illustration and is not designed to be exhaustive.

Intolerable harm

Products must be designed to avoid foreseeable harm to customers (PRIN 2A.2.10) through, amongst other things, "taking appropriate action to mitigate the risk of actual or foreseeable harm, including for example by: (i) updating or otherwise amending the design of the product or distribution strategy; (ii) updating information about a product or updating investment advice; (iii) ensuring that retail customers do not face unreasonable barriers (including unreasonable additional costs), for example when they want to switch products or providers or to complain; (iv) allowing time and support for retail customers to find suitable alternatives where a product is withdrawn".

To achieve the above and successfully mitigate foreseeable harm, one method a firm can use is to identify the point at which harm becomes intolerable for a customer. When determining intolerability, the bar should be set low, as the Duty implies the need to do as much as possible to remove harms altogether (where the harm is not an inherent risk associated with the product). However, the wording of PRIN 2A.2.10 does give us confidence that the FCA does not expect harms to be removed altogether, instead mitigated as far as is reasonably practical.

Identifying where harms breach this level is a helpful step for firms, both as part of the product approval but also to set KRIs that can be used for ongoing outcomes monitoring.

Form of Assessment

There are no requirements as to the form of the product approval assessment, however most manufacturers will create a checklist including the content as described in this section. The checklist must be completed, with supporting evidence, and reviewed by the relevant governing body prior to sign-off.

5.3: Output

The output from the product approval is the distribution strategy, which is essentially a group of policies, procedures and working documents detailing how the product is to be distributed. The scope of the strategy, however, goes beyond the sale of the product to include all aspects of the customer journey. As a result, the policies, procedures and working documents should include post-sale support, key communication points and customer support provisions.

Working documents expected as part of the distribution strategy include any scripts, guidelines and training materials.

Overall, manufacturers are making sure the product is designed to support good outcomes and the associated service provision is aligned with this aim. The output, as detailed in earlier sections, will depend on the role of the firm in the distribution chain, the impact of the product's inherent product risk and nature of the product.

Example

A firm sells a high-risk investment product on an execution only basis, they identify and mitigate potential harms during the sales process, such as ensuring the customer watches an educational video, however they also need to identify post-sale risks and likely support required by its customer base.

In this case, the typical customer is reasonably affluent, educated and experienced with financial services. As a result, the post-sale support can be provided through a mix of written correspondence designed to provide timely information, especially where action is required, and online support. The online support consists of both information (such as frequently asked question pages) and self-help tools to enable the customer to take their required action. There is also a call centre option available for those who require additional support.

Whilst the support is generally sufficient for the target market, due to the high-risk nature of the product, additional features may well be deemed necessary including the ability to switch should the customer's ability to absorb risk change after the point of sale.

This is one example of many that could be cited, it is designed to highlight the level of thought which needs to be given to the requirements of customers and that a range of solutions should be considered.

5.4: Distributors

Strictly speaking the product approval requirements in PRIN 2A.3 do not apply to distributors, instead, as mentioned, they are required to follow the instructions of the manufacturer – the instructions created as part of the manufacturer's approval process. This requires a level of information sharing between both parties. The process for this will usually entail:

1. Contractual requirements to follow the distribution instructions as well as to share information with the manufacturer, such as charges applied to the customer's account, or, where the manufacturer does not interact with the customer, information about the characteristics of those who have bought the product as well as product performance data. The latter enables the manufacturer to complete accurate outcomes monitoring, value assessments and product reviews.

2. Due diligence undertaken on the distributor, ensuring they are capable of meeting the distribution instructions.

3. Detailed distribution instructions, explaining the product features, intended target market, negative target market, requirements in relation to financial promotions, and required steps when selling the product.

Despite the requirement mainly resting on the manufacturer, often distributors apply their own version of a product approval process. This process is a helpful set of standards for those working in distributors, providing a step-by-step process to ensure they have gathered enough information to properly understand the product, the needs of the target market, foreseeable harms and the requirements of the manufacturer and then to create the distribution process, documentation, and training required. Additionally, it can be used to ensure the distributor performs their own target market analysis, bolstering / challenging that of the manufacturer. In practice the FCA requires distributors to take a level of responsibility for the product they distribute; simply and blindly relying on the manufacturer's instructions will not suffice. This is demonstrated through the authorisation process, where new applicants, including distributors, are challenged to take responsibility. The FCA expects all firms to understand their target market's characteristics, needs and to take steps to help customers achieve their goals.

Once again, the process does not stop at implementation. Distributors will need monitoring arrangements in place to assess how successful their approval process has been in implementing the manufacturer's instructions. As part of monitoring, it is good practice for distributors to perform their own analysis of customer outcomes – informing the manufacturer where they identify problems.

5.5: Vulnerable Customers

Products must be designed to support vulnerable customers; it cannot not be underestimated just how much focus the FCA expects on this requirement. PRIN 2A.3.4R is the rule creating the requirement to complete product approvals and this one rule mentions vulnerability three times, more than any other specific requirement. At a high-level, it requires that firms assess the risks to customers with characteristics of vulnerability, take into account the needs of vulnerable customers when designing the product, and ensure the design of the product does not disadvantage vulnerable customers.

The focus on vulnerability will be of no surprise to knowledgeable compliance professionals, since the release of the FCA's Vulnerable Customer Guidance in February 2021 there has been an obvious drive to improve financial services for such customers, manifesting in an undercurrent to other policy statements, rules, and guidance. Nevertheless, the Consumer Duty has taken it to a new level.

As such most manufacturers will have a separate section within their product approval, considering the likely vulnerabilities in the target market and the foreseeable harms which can derive from them. Identifying the vulnerabilities likely to be present in the target market can be a difficult task, most will rely on historical data for similar products to help ascertain the characteristics of the customer base. However, this approach does have two limitations, firstly it assumes that historic data gathering has been accurate and extensive enough to properly identify vulnerability in the market. Secondly, organisations will apply shorter data retention periods to certain vulnerability data, specifically data, which is special category data, as a result not all data may be available at the point in time the approval occurs.

Data Protection, as set out in the UK General Data Protection Regulation (UK GDPR), should not be allowed to prevent all data sharing and/or analysis for this purpose. UK GDPR requires data controllers to consider their basis for processing (recording, maintaining, using or sending) data and to ensure that it is fair and reasonable to do so. Controllers must have a basis for doing so under Article 6 (for personal data) and Article 9 (for special categories of data such as data relating to health); in financial services this is often explicit consent, although there are further bases that can be considered. Once the criteria to process the data has been met, the organisation may record it and use it for the purposes that it has been processed for, such as assisting the customer. Where this has happened, it can be freely used as part of any analysis under the Consumer Duty. In line with the data protection principles, data should only be used if it is necessary to do so and there is no need to include data which may enable the customer to be identified (name or address) when analysing a target market's characteristics, therefore these elements should be redacted. This supports the principle that data must only be kept for as long as is necessary, as the retention period of vulnerability data ends, the data which has been pseudonymised does not need to be deleted as this is exempt from the requirement to do so. Instead, it remains data which may be used for statistical purposes, such as consumer Duty assessments.

CHAPTER SIX

FAIR VALUE ASSESSMENTS: MANUFACTURERS

6.1: Assessment Trigger

As one of the four outcomes, 'price and value' requires an assessment of its own: a value assessment. PRIN 2A.4.3R requires an assessment of value to take place for a new product or a 'significant adaptation of a product'.

In the case of fair value assessments, a 'significant adaptation of a product' would include where:

- The target market has changed.
- Key features of the product have been added or removed.
- Any other change to the terms and conditions.

As we will cover in the next section, the FCA also require a fresh assessment where market changes impact upon the value received by the customer, such as the addition of new, competing products on the market, technological innovation, or economic changes. This is illustrated from the savings market as the Bank of England raised the base rate between April 2022 and August 2023 you would expect to see the interest rates paid on savings accounts to increase at a similar rate. Failure to do so would, under the Duty, leave the lender offering a product of unfair value.

Because the assessment triggers are similar to those for the product approval, common practice is to include the value assessment as a section within the product approval. A standalone assessment should also be maintained as there can be triggers which solely impact the value of the product or service.

6.2: Regulatory action

Cash-Savings

In the weeks following the Duty's implementation, the FCA demonstrated their willingness to take firms to task where fair value is not provided to customers. On 31st July 2023 the FCA set out a 14-point action plan for Banks and Building Societies providing cash-saving products. The plan is devised to work alongside and guide value assessments by requiring a fresh assessment each time there is a base rate change. It also asks firms to take a number of other steps including the need to review their performance where a customer switches from one cash ISA to another, as well as requiring firms to analyse the difference between on-sale and off-sale products, challenging firms to explain how large differences offer fair value. Once the Duty was fully in force, the FCA soon followed up on this action plan writing to the Banks and Building Societies offering the lowest savings rates asking them to justify the rate and to provide copies of their value assessments.

As part of the action plan Sheldon Mills, Executive Director of Consumers and Competition at the FCA, said:

> *'We want a competitive cash savings market that delivers better deals for savers, where interest rates are reviewed quickly following base rate changes and firms prompt savers to switch to accounts paying higher rates.*
>
> *'We welcome the progress that has been made so far but this needs to speed up. We will be using the Consumer Duty to ensure this is the case – with firms required to prove to us that they are offering their customers fair value.'*

(*https://www.fca.org.uk/news/press-releases/action-plan-cash-savings*)

In December 2023 the FCA provided an update on its work in the market. This outlined that improvements had been made in the timeliness of passing on higher interest rates to customers, however this update did state "*Following the introduction of the Consumer Duty, we requested 9 firms to provide us with their fair value assessments (FVAs) for their lowest paying (on-sale) easy access savings accounts. Our review of these FVAs has raised important questions about how firms assess value. We will work closely with firms over the next few months to ensure their assessments are fit for purpose. We remain committed to taking robust action against firms who cannot demonstrate fair value.*"
(https://www.fca.org.uk/data/fca-update-cash-savings-december-2023)

The cash-savings example is demonstrative of the agility and vigour the FCA now expects of firms in relation to their value assessments. Manufacturers must have systems in place to identify indicators that a review must take place, ensuring that it can be completed without delay and savings passed on to customers. Furthermore, when reviews are undertaken, they must be data driven and detailed enough to properly understand the level of value provided to customers. High level statements confirming a belief that the product offers value is not sufficient.

Gap-Insurance

Another example is that of GAP insurance. On 9 February 2024 the FCA announced that multiple suppliers of Guaranteed Asset Protection (GAP) insurance had agreed to pause sales, following a request from the regulator. GAP insurance is typically sold alongside car finance. It covers the difference between a vehicle's purchase price or outstanding finance and its current market value, in the event it is written off before finance has been repaid.

In an example of the regulator using its regulatory return data, the FCA noted that only 6% of the amount customers pay in premiums were paid out in claims, far lower than most other insurance products. This, together with examples seen by the FCA where 70% of premiums were paid in commission to those involved in selling the GAP products, led the FCA to the obvious conclusion that customers were not receiving fair value. The FCA identified concerns with the design of GAP insurance across all distribution channels and therefore required firms to make changes.

This example demonstrates the FCA flexing their muscles, highlighting the aggressive approach (preventing 80% of the market from selling a product) they are willing to take where fair value is not provided. There are two key learning points. The first is just how important it is for organisations, including brokers, to take these requirements with the utmost seriousness. Secondly, a more technical point, is to include the level of commission provided to others in the distribution chain when conducting the review.

6.3: Assessing Value

Overview

There are several approaches a manufacturer can take to complete a value assessment. Competitor price comparison is one useful model, another is 'price to cost justification' where the manufacturer justifies the prices they are charging customers through identifying their costs to create and deliver the product. A third model is customer segmentation. Customer segmentation works by identifying groups of customers who purchase the product, using the defining characteristics of the class of customers to create groups, then performing an analysis to determine whether any groups of customers pay more for the same service or, importantly, pay the same amount but receive a lesser service or benefit.

The characteristics that can be used for the latter are wide-ranging, from demographic based traits through to the distribution channel the customer used to purchase the product. There is no right answer, segments will depend on the nature of the product itself, although it is worth pointing out that the FCA has been sceptical of value assessments which have been mainly based around competitor comparisons.

What is clear is that the manufacturer must ensure they always include the key features and benefits of the product, its limitations, and the characteristics of those in the target market when assessing how these characteristics may, or do, impact on the value received by those accessing the product. When doing so it is important to ascertain whether any specific characteristics, including vulnerabilities, have prevented customers from accessing all or some of the product's value.

To ensure that segmentation is able to inform the value assessment, the manufacturer must ensure that they always include the key features and benefits of the product, the product's target market, and the target market's characteristics. The goal is to assess how these characteristics may – or do – impact on the value received by those in the target market. To do so it is important to ascertain whether any specific characteristics have prevented customers from accessing all or some of the product's value. When assessing whether any characteristics have an impact on the value received, vulnerabilities must be assessed.

Assessing Value

As there are several methods that can be used to assess value, this section intends to suggest some areas for review, rather than provide a comprehensive explanation of value assessments. Almost all manufacturers will be able to identify the behavioural biases within their target market as well as any cognitive limitations, and these are key areas to assess value. For example, a manufacturer may ask themselves whether cognitive or behavioural biases of customers impact on the value of the product to the customer. Perhaps the customer's cognitive issues mean it is challenging for that individual to communicate with the product supplier. Each year the product supplier assesses the cost of their product and, often, increases the price at renewal. To do so, they write to customers to explain the price rise, giving them an option to call to discuss should they be unable to afford the increase. Whilst the firm may be acting in good faith, attempting to support customers in financial difficulties, in effect, this policy could result in individuals with communication difficulties, such as those with certain cognitive problems or some vulnerable customers, choosing not to call and, instead resigning themselves to accepting higher charges. This issue could be identified as part of the value assessment process through analysing the price paid by different segments of customers, identifying those segments that are paying more and running a root cause analysis.

To measure value, a balancing test must be conducted, on the one side the price paid by the customer and on the other the product or service provided by the firm. This is because value can be measured by both cost to the customer and by their ability to utilise all aspects of the product. Therefore, firms should ask themselves if any aspects or limitations of the product prevents the average target customer from fully enjoying the product?

Looking firstly at the price paid by the customer, this will include monetary payments, but the FCA has explained multiple times that price paid goes beyond this to also include time, effort, and other non-financial payments such as data, provided by the customer. A compliant value assessment will add-up these monetary and non-financial payments and weigh them against the product or service provided.

Conditional fees are an area that have received much FCA attention, through their webinars and final guidance. Such fees include charges for late payments, administrative charges or other similar fees based on a specific event occurring. The regulator's expectations are quite clear; the charge levied to the customer must represent the true cost to the business. This effectively bans profiteering from contingent fees. The value assessment is the place to set out contingent fees potentially payable on the product, with a calculation demonstrating the cost to the manufacturer and that the amount charged to the customer does not exceed this cost.

PRIN 2.4.9G offers suggestions for data that can be reviewed when determining fair value. Suggestions include the cost of manufacturing the product, market rate for comparable products, whether there are other products in the market or offered by the manufacturer themselves which offer similar benefits for a lower price. Whilst this section does not ban differential pricing in the market, it is advisable that firms that do charge more for a similar product, have a strong justification for doing so recorded in their value assessment. For example, providing an enhanced customer support, such as the support facility we described in the credit repair example, could justify charging more for the product.

Other factors

If there are different fees charged to customers depending on the distribution channel, i.e. online vs. face to face, the difference must be justified. For example, face to face attracting a higher charge due to the bespoke advice provided.

Remember the assessment must cover any fees which may be added throughout the life of the product, those only considering charges at the first point of purchase will not be compliant. The example cited in earlier chapters where the FCA wrote to a small number of wealth managers with a series of questions in relation to the cost of annual reviews and whether the customer received what they paid for is pertinent to value assessments. Whilst this information request was not strictly covering value assessments it does serve to demonstrate the regulator's approach to fair value, ensuring that value is measured throughout the life cycle and customers receive what they have paid for, or a refund.

Where organisations collaborate to manufacture a product, such as in a co-manufacturer relationship, a written agreement must set out who is responsible for ensuring fair value and that the value assessment is completed.

Ultimately, when measuring the value of the product, manufacturers must be mindful of the core expectation of PRIN 2A.4.1R, which states "For the purposes of this outcome: (1) value is the relationship between the amount paid by a retail customer for the product and the benefits they can reasonably expect to get from the product; and (2) a product provides fair value where the amount paid for the product is reasonable relative to the benefits of the product."

When assessing the total cost of the product, the entire distribution chain must be included; it is imperative to include any charges applied by third parties, such as those distributing the product (i.e. brokers). As ever with the Consumer Duty, the lens to look through is not simply 'what have we done' but 'what does the customer experience', therefore if a broker, or other third party, adds a fee this must be included in the value assessment. Manufacturers must ensure they have the relevant arrangements in place to share this data in a timely manner.

The obvious focus is on commissions paid and there have been two examples which help to highlight the consideration firms must have in this area. The first is in relation to price increases during the period of high inflation between 2023 and 2024, where commissions for products such as investment management were set at a certain percentage of the value of the product. But if that product has increased in price by 10%, can the recipient of the commission justify receiving 10% more revenue? In other words, do they undertake 10% more work or have they experienced a comparable increase in cost. The other example is from vehicle finance, as explained in the next section.

Examining Vehicle Finance

Discretionary commission arrangements allowed dealerships – the brokers – discretion to add any level of commission they wanted, as long as the customer accepted the overall price at the point of sale. Such arrangements leave manufacturers vulnerable for a number of reasons, which should be called out in the value assessment review. Firstly, there is the obvious issue of a lack of consistency. Two customers, purchasing the same product (the loan), for the same vehicle and amount, may pay very different amounts depending on which dealership they purchase from, despite the dealerships both offering the exact same service. Additionally, those customers less willing or able to negotiate may well pay more for exactly the same product and service. It is clear to see how some vulnerable customers may well fall into this category of customer.

The second issue is the level of oversight, or potential for lack of it, from the manufacturer. Historically they may have been unaware of the fees levied by the dealer, with such fees rolled into the total cost of credit and therefore unable to gain any sense of whether customers are receiving fair value or are being overcharged by dealers.

These issues get to the centre of the price and value outcome. No longer can lenders, or other manufacturers, have arrangements in place which leave them unable to measure the fairness of charges let alone ascertain what the customer has actually been charged. There is now a responsibility to be interested in what the customer is paying. Furthermore, they must also ensure charging structures are consistent between customers in the absence of objectively justifiable reasons for differential pricing, such as credit risk.

Assessing value summary

In summary the following are considerations to take into account when assessing value:

1. Manufacturers must ensure they have sight of the final, and total, price paid by the customer through ensuring distribution arrangements enable transparency through the sharing of information.

2. Consistent pricing is required, ensuring customers are not charged different amounts due to the distribution channel or specific distributor.

3. The value for money the customer gets when compared to similar products in the market, or through reviewing how much of the overall cost of the product is actually for the product itself.

4. Reasonableness of commission payments, if they make up the majority of the fee, then they are clearly not good value for money.

5. Whether the customer getting everything they paid for i.e. are they using all elements of the service and if not, have they been refunded?

6. Are certain groups of customers, such as vulnerable customers, using less of the product's features?

7. Finally, are groups of customers, such as longstanding customers, getting different outcomes compared to others, such as paying more for less?

Duration of the Assessment

The manufacturer must, at the point of conducting a value assessment, consider how long the assessment will be applicable for. PRIN 2A.4.5 states that "In ensuring that a product provides fair value, a manufacturer must be satisfied that this will be the case from the point at which the manufacturer completes the assessment for a reasonably foreseeable period, including, where the product is one that renews, following renewal" and PRIN 2A.4.2 requires assessments to be revisited at reasonable intervals. In determining a 'reasonably foreseeable period' the manufacturer should have regard to the length of time they would expect a retail customer to maintain the product, including the likelihood of renewal.

Packaged Products

Where a product is intended to be provided with one or more other products, a manufacturer must ensure that each component product, and the package as a whole, provides fair value to retail customers in the target market. This is the requirement under PRIN 2A.4.7R.

6.4: Distributors

The requirement to conduct value assessments rests on the manufacturer rather than the distributor, however the requirements clearly impact distributors.

As with product approvals, distributors are under a duty to follow and comply with the manufacturer's distribution instructions, except where the distributor identifies non-compliance with the Duty, such as a lack of value. Following each value assessment, including those conducted when a new product or service is created, a detailed set of instructions should follow. Those instructions will explain the target market and provide a set of requirements in relation to financial promotions, ensuring they are understandable for the intended market and targeted towards that market. It will also comprise steps to be completed during on-boarding to ensure the product is suitable for the customer. In their round these requirements are also designed to help ensure fair value, the theory being that if the incorrect customer purchases the product, they would be less likely to be able to utilise its benefits and therefore would receive less for their money.

The above paragraph is written on the assumption that the distributor is selling the product or service to the customer. This may not always be the case, such as those providing non-sales advice services, customer support services or complaints handling, to name a few alternatives. The principles for these types of services are the same, with the manufacturer providing relevant instructions and the distributor taking care to follow them.

The instruction from the manufacturer is also likely to comprise a framework of charges the distributor can levy, if any. These charges will have been carefully crafted to avoid the pitfalls mentioned in this chapter, again the distributor's role is to comply with this framework.

Another focus for those distributing the product is quality of their service. The charges they add, including where these charges are not paid directly by the customer but instead contribute to the overall cost of the service, must be justifiable. Products are provided with either an express or implied level of service, where firm's fall below the standard expected there is, in turn, an impact on the value received by the customer. Distributors must therefore take steps to ensure their service meets the quality standards set by the manufacturer or enhanced standards of their own. Such steps may include a quality monitoring and assurance framework overseeing the essential processes of the organisation. Evidencing quality through the recording the result of the framework is obviously essential from the point of view of demonstrating compliance to the regulator but it can provide valuable MI for manufacturers when reviewing price and value, perhaps even indicating the distributor should be paid more – it should therefore be seen as an opportunity to drive income.

Aside from following the instructions of the manufacturer, distributors are expected to accept a level of responsibility for the value received by customers. A starting point is to check the manufacturer's instructions, taking steps to understand how they have formulated their value assessments and whether there are any major faults, specifically in relation to the service the distributor is providing. For example, if the manufacturer gives the distributor permission to levy a fee which is clearly disproportionate to the service provided, the FCA would expect the distributor not to apply the fee in its entirety, instead ascertaining for themselves a fair fee to charge. The distributor must also then inform the manufacturer, so they are able to take steps to review their decision. If the distributor was simply to apply to unreasonable fee, they would be unable to rely on the defence they followed the manufacturer's instructions.

CHAPTER SEVEN

PRODUCT REVIEWS: OPEN MANUFACTURERS

7.1: Triggers

Introduction

The product approval process and value assessment are intended to ensure that products work well for customers. However, a measure of real-world performance is required to ascertain whether the design has, in fact, been successful. Outcomes monitoring is a continuous review of whether products are working well for customers. To support this the FCA requires a further assessment, a 'product review'. The best way to understand a product review is to consider it as a 'back-stop' performance check, similar to a third line audit review. The product review is an opportunity to pause, reflect on the intention of the product or service, and formally assess whether it has achieved those objectives. In doing so it is imperative to assess the outcomes *actually received* by customers, as such, most organisations will be able to lean on the outcomes monitoring data produced since the previous review.

Timing

The obligation to conduct product reviews rests with the manufacturer. It is PRIN 2A.3.7R which sets out the timing requirement, stating "A manufacturer must regularly review its products". Aside from this statement and the requirement to conduct reviews as part of the implementation of the Duty (outlined below) there is little further guidance setting out how often reviews should be undertaken.

Timing is, therefore, not the primary catalyst of the review, instead "any event that could materially affect the potential risk to the target market" (PRIN 2A.3.7R) is the driver for a review, with the caveat that in the absence of an event, reviews should take place at 'regular' intervals. The definition of 'regular' in this case would depend upon the product and business type.

Implementation of the Duty

A central pillar of the FCA's implementation plan was the completion of the product reviews which were designed to make manufacturers look at their products through a 'consumer Duty lens', which should provide them with a clear view of the outcomes that customers receive. The final rules and guidance were released on 27 July 2022 giving manufacturers until 30 April 2023 to complete their open product reviews and 31 July 2023 to take any remedial actions identified. Furthermore, firms were given until 31 July 2024 to complete closed product reviews, including taking any mitigating actions.

7.2: Content

The sections of PRIN leading the content requirements are:

> 2A.3.7R: (1) whether the product meets the identified needs, characteristics and objectives of the target market, including identified needs, characteristics and objectives of retail customers in the target market with characteristics of vulnerability; and (2) whether the intended distribution strategy remains appropriate, including whether the product is being distributed to the target market or, instead, reaching retail customers outside the target market.

> 2A.3.12R: (1) A manufacturer must select distribution channels that are appropriate for the target market. (2) A manufacturer must provide each distributor with

adequate information in good time to enable it to comply with the rules applicable to it in this section. (3) The information to be made available under (2) includes all appropriate information regarding the product and the product approval process from time to time to enable the distributor to comply with PRIN 2A.3.16R.

Whilst PRIN 2A.3.9R is not strictly a requirement in relation to product reviews, the product review, alongside product approvals, is an opportunity to meet the provision. This section requires manufacturers to test their products appropriately and, if taken together with the product review requirements, provides guidance on the content of the reviews, namely:

(1) assess whether the product meets the identified needs and objectives of the target market.

(2) assess whether the characteristics of customers entering into the product impact on the product's ability to meet the needs and objectives outlined in (1).

(3) when assessing the characteristics of customers, vulnerable customers must be included in the assessment.

It further clarifies that testing must be conducted in a qualitative manner as well as quantitative.

It therefore follows that the content of an open product review can include:

1. A detailed product description enabling the distributor to meet their obligations under PRIN 2A.3.16. It should therefore include key features such as interest rates, terms available, fixed / flexible term, secured / unsecured, open credit, advised / non-advised etc. together with the intended benefits of the product, natural limitations and risks.

2. The target market the product is designed for, including characteristics, needs and objectives of the group of customers the product / service is designed to meet. Characteristics such as age, financial experience, education level, wealth / income can be included.

3. it is recommended that vulnerable customers are reviewed separately to the main target market, through focusing on actual characteristics of vulnerability experienced by customers within the target market. This can be conducted on a cohort basis rather than on an individual customer basis. Firms should be looking to identify the common vulnerabilities in the market such as language, literacy, age, health, and experience. The review should then be able to identify the risks to vulnerable customers in the target market.

4. The distribution strategy, specifically why the distribution strategy is appropriate for the customers within the target market and how it meets their needs including customers with characteristics of vulnerability.

5. The testing the product has undergone, ensuring it covers communication, customer support and whether any steps put in place to mitigate the risk of harm (such as friction) have been successful.

6. A summary stating whether the product is producing good outcomes for customers and, if not, the steps to be taken.

Form of Assessment

The assessment can be completed in any form, this is not dictated by the regulations. Almost all firms have created a standard product review template, taking the format of a table with the above content listed.

7.3: Identifying poor faith

Good faith extends to all aspects of the customer journey, clearly the product must be designed to the standards of good faith and the role of product reviews is to ascertain whether this has been successfully achieved. In doing so the following can be reviewed:

- Whether features of the product have been designed to avoid exploiting behavioural biases. Exploitation can range from the design of financial promotions to discouraging customers to make a complaint, or switch product.

- Whether the firm has purposefully added variations to their products to make them more difficult to compare to other products on the market.

- If the products are not offering fair value, whether action has been taken to rectify the problem and offer redress.

- If genuine attempts have been made to ensure communication is understandable for the target market.

- Has communication been designed to encourage customers to make well informed decisions, in their best interests or has it been designed solely to increase the profitability of the firm.

- Whether the firm's culture supports the Duty.

Poor faith can be baked into the culture of an organisation or individuals within that organisation, often without realising it. Financial promotions is an area repeatedly referred to in the final guidance but it does provide opportunity to explore exactly what is meant by poor faith. The FCA's final guidance is awash with examples of poor faith in financial promotions, including promotions which take advantage of the behavioural bias of customers through relaying the potential benefits of the product over and above the risks associated. An example is a social media advert for a peer-to-peer investment. A lack of good faith in the promotion could prominently feature a positive looking image, visually depicting an individual making excellent returns and supporting the image with wording to the effect of "invest in peer-to-peer today and start your journey. Thousands of people see staggering returns". In comparison a well-balanced promotion may include the following wording "invest in peer-to-peer today and start your journey. Don't invest unless you're prepared to lose all of your investment, this is a high-risk investment." This may well be supported by a more balanced image. One promotion is designed solely to make sales, whereas the 'good faith' example is designed to give customers the right information to make an informed decision.

Achieving well-balanced, good faith promotions on a consistent basis requires marketing departments, sales, operations and senior management to be aligned with compliance and the ethos of the Duty. This can be difficult to accomplish because marketing, sales and operations are traditionally focused on making sales, increasing income and making profit. To align their culture with the goals of the Duty, the factors causing the 'sales-first' point of view must be identified and tackled.

Judging the performance of a marketing team by assessing the number of sales attained from their financial promotions is a major root cause of a culture which fails to properly support good faith. With the incentive to simply attract as many customers as possible, the marketing team will push the content of their adverts as far as they can. They will try to highlight the potential benefits of the product whilst taking attention away from the risks and limitations as much as they can, because this approach achieves the greatest number of sales. Let's call this a 'sales-first' approach.

Senior management have often felt this approach aligned with their goals, increasing sales which in turn increases turnover and profit. Those senior managers need to ask themselves whether the 'sales-first' approach actually does achieve their goals. Society is becoming increasingly litigious. Driven by the claims management sector, customers expect compensation where they have been wronged. Regulatory standards are aligned with this 'compensation culture' with firms expected to issue redress when harm has been identified. For example, FS 22/5 states "Firms must take appropriate action where their review identifies that a product or service does not provide fair value. This may include amending the benefits or price of a product or service so that it provides fair value, withdrawing the product, or where consumers have suffered harm, providing redress." (FG 22/5, p.67) and "If, for example, a firm identifies that a systemic or recurring issue in the delivery of its consumer support prevented customers from utilising a product or service as anticipated, it should act in good faith and consider whether remedial action would be appropriate. This might include providing redress commensurate with the benefit that was difficult to utilise or proactively contacting customers to explain the issue and the steps they can take to fully utilise the product or service." (FG22/5, p106). The latter example demonstrating another aspect of good faith, pro-actively offering redress where it is due. As compensation culture has grown, senior managers are beginning to recognise the importance of protecting the business against such claims. It follows that it is no longer in the business' interest to allow a 'sales-first' culture which demonstrably lacks good faith in financial promotions (or other areas) creating a risk of claims and/or regulatory action due to a breach of the Consumer Duty.

One does not have to look too far to see examples of firms collapsing due to the activities of claims management companies. Wonga, for example, were subject to criticism from the FCA in relation to their products – claims management companies then began to push complaints to the Financial Ombudsman Service on behalf of their customers, often advertising the service to specifically target Wonga. The high levels of complaints, Ombudsman case-fees, and redress to pay meant the firm was no longer viable and it was placed into liquidation.

Moving beyond financial promotions

As highlighted, culture is key, and of course culture goes beyond financial promotions: "Firms also need to ensure that their culture supports and is conducive to their staff acting in good faith. A firm is unlikely to be able to act in good faith if it uses staff incentives, performance management or remuneration structures which are likely to cause detriment to their customers. Firms should have adequate arrangements in place that can help to detect and manage the risk of non-compliance with regulatory obligations arising from their remuneration or performance management practices" (FG 22/5, p.30). It is imperative to look at all business processes, from those considered to be 'customer facing' through to human resources, in order to assess whether the process is consistent with acting in good faith, or whether it is likely to encourage a behaviour which is not aligned with the customers' best interests.

There is an imbalance in the bargaining position when customers deal with financial services firms. Generally speaking, customers do not have access to the advice and resources of a firm nor do they possess the relevant knowledge and expertise. It is therefore reasonable to expect that firms operate openly and fairly with customers, enabling them to make effective decisions. This requires firms to be open and honest with customers. Section 5.9 of the FCA's final guidance highlights this point "A firm would not be acting in good faith where it fails to take account of customers' interests, for example in the way it designs a product or presents information. Seeking to exploit consumers' lack of knowledge and understanding would also be a clear sign a firm is not acting in good faith. This would include seeking to exploit customers' behavioural biases, such as tendencies to be influenced by the way things are presented, overvaluing immediate impacts and undervaluing future ones or attaching less weight to effects that are further off, such as termination or renewal fees." (FG 22/5, p.29)

The relationship between open product reviews and the good faith rule is excellently summarised by the following statement "If a firm continues to sell a product it knows to be causing harm, it is also likely to be acting in bad faith." (FG22/5, p.28)

7.4: Identifying foreseeable harms

PRIN 2A.3.4R requires manufacturers to avoid "causing foreseeable harm in the target market" as part of the design and distribution of products or services. The requirement applies to product approvals but equally to product reviews.

As a manufacturer steps back and reviews whether the product has functioned in the real world as it was thought it would, the core of this review is to identify harms which have actually occurred, take steps to prevent such harms from occurring in the future, and put things right with affected customers. In accordance with PRIN 2A.3.8 manufacturers must, where they identify there are aspects of the product which may harm customers, take appropriate action to mitigate the situation and prevent any further harm; and where appropriate, promptly inform other relevant persons in the distribution chain about the circumstances that led to action being taken and the remedial action taken.

The role of foreseeable harm is further emphasised in the final guidance, where it is highlighted that it is the responsibility of firms to avoid foreseeable harm which could be caused by their acts or omissions. This includes ensuring that no aspect of their design, terms and conditions, marketing, sale of and support for their products or services cause foreseeable harm whether intentionally designed to do so or not. In this way foreseeable harm is different from good faith as there does not need to be an element of intention. It does not matter if the harm was not identifiable when the product was created, instead when the harm is actually identified – perhaps during the product review – the regulator would "expect firms to take appropriate action to mitigate the risk of actual or foreseeable harm" (FG 22/5, p.32). An example is that of any advice provided to a customer. If the advice provider becomes aware that the advice is no longer suitable, it would be prudent to contact the customer to issue new and updated advice.

The guidance provides insight on when a harm is foreseeable, stating "Whether harm is considered foreseeable would depend on whether a prudent firm acting reasonably would be able to predict or expect the ultimately harmful result of their action or omission in connection with the product or service." (FG22/5, p.31). Examples are provided in the guidance which include processes which make it difficult for a customer to cancel a product which isn't right for them because the firm's processes are unclear or difficult to navigate, customers receiving higher than necessary charges because they don't understand the charging structure, and customers becoming victims of scams due to a firm's inadequate systems to design, test, and measure the effectiveness of scam warnings. The FCA does, however, go on to state "firms are only responsible for addressing the risk of harm when it is reasonably foreseeable at the time, considering what a firm knows, or could reasonably be expected to have known." (FG22/5, p.32). There is, therefore, a subjective element to consider when deciding what 'foreseeable' is, including the level of information gathered by the firm and whether the information gathered is reasonable taking into account the organisation's size and nature.

There are key harms which should be actively looked for during the review, including examples of behavioural bias causing detriment to customers, a lack of understanding of key product features such as the charging structure, and new or emerging harms.

To identify new or emerging harms, there is a number of resources that can be utilised. Externally manufacturers are able to use regulatory communications such as 'Dear CEO' letters, guidance documents, or Ombudsman decisions. Press reports and economic trends may also be used. For example, a retail bank offering mortgages linked to the Bank of England base rate should recognise changes in the base rate as a potential harm. Internally manufacturers may analyse complaints data, MI or customer feedback to continually look for new themes playing out amongst customers which may suggest a trend for a new harm.

Where foreseeable harms have been identified, there are several tools which can be used to mitigate the impact of the harms crystallising, the tools often manifesting in two of the other outcomes, communication and customer service. From a communication perspective, timely calls to action and pro-actively communicating key risks and events can assist. Consumer support tools may also be used. These can include timely access to support features like call centres or online services, a flexible approach to customers enabling them to take action should it be required, and friction in the customer journey to slow the customer experience where a decision is made which, if the customer makes the incorrect decision, poor outcomes could follow.

7.5: Enable and support customers to pursue their financial objectives

As with foreseeable harm, the requirement to support customers to achieve good financial outcomes must be considered at all stages of the product life cycle. From a product governance point of view, this requires manufacturers to create products and support features at the design stage to support financial outcomes and then to review the success of the product at achieving this goal. This is the product review.

Again, in a similar vein to the foreseeable harm cross-cutting rule, the starting point is not that the manufacturer must remove all possibility of poor financial outcomes, instead they are tasked with enabling and supporting customers to make decisions which support their financial objectives. Many of the actions which will create this environment are the same actions which demonstrate both good faith and avoiding foreseeable harm, such as providing timely information in a way that is understandable for the customer and/or target market. Other supportive actions may include the use of positive friction to reduce decisions made on impulse and product flexibility enabling the product to change, or the customer to change product, where their financial objectives change.

Another important step which can be taken is to consider the different needs of vulnerable customers, focusing on the impact their vulnerability may have on decision making and taking steps to provide additional support.

The level of support that can be offered by a firm will vary depending on the type of service offered, the FCA highlight this in their final guidance, but it is also highlighted in PRIN 2A.2.16. Essentially where a firm is acting on an advised basis, they have the responsibility to properly understand the customer's individual circumstances, objectives, capabilities (both financial and non-financial) and provide bespoke advice which, if followed, provides the best possible opportunity for that customer to achieve their objective. This does not mean the product must then be successful in doing so. Although this statement feels counterintuitive, there is inherent risk in certain products, such as investments which can result in the customer's original objectives not being met. The FCA, however, is clear; it is not the role of the manufacturer (or distributor) to remove the inherent risk, instead it is incumbent on those firms to ensure the customer is fully aware of the risks involved and, fully accepts them when making the purchase.

Where the firm is providing a non-advised service, the firm can presume the objective of the customer is to use and enjoy the full benefit of the product or service. It follows that the manufacturer must ensure the product functions as the customer has been led to expect, communications support customers' understanding of the product, and there is sufficient flexibility built into the product to allow it to be amended should the customer's circumstances change. There is still a level of responsibility to support the financial objectives of customers, although it is not as tailored as it is for advised services.

Product reviews should review a range of MI, including where customers move away from the product. Where possible the reason for their doing so should be analysed and used to identify product improvements and to consider further support which can be provided to customers who have closed the product or moved away. One example is signposting to agencies which could provide support or guidance, useful in the event that findings show that customers were confused about changes to the product or about how to use particular elements of the product.

An obvious step that can be taken to help compliance with this rule is to remove any charges for moving or switching accounts, as the charges are barriers to supporting customers' financial objectives. Ensuring that consumer support enables consumers to fully use the products and services they buy and supports them in acting in their own interests is another key step: this includes avoiding 'sludge' in the design of consumer journeys, which uses friction to prevent consumers from taking actions such as cancelling a product or accessing support. Sludge practices usually benefit the firm over the consumer, and common examples include needing the customer to visit a branch in person to close their account, including hidden fees such as early closure fees, or aggressive retention tactics, including repeated calls from customer service to try to convince the customer to keep their account before the firm will close the account.

The product review should identify the actual outcomes received by customers, evaluating whether their financial objectives were met and setting out steps to improve the service going forward. As always with the Duty, where poor outcomes are identified, redress should follow.

7.6: Distributors

PRIN 2A.3.14R is the requirement for distributors. They must maintain, operate, and review distribution arrangements to ensure that they avoid causing and/or mitigate foreseeable harm, properly manage conflicts of interest and ensure the needs, characteristics and objectives of the target market are taken into account when designing the distribution strategy. Whilst PRIN 2A.3.14R mostly pertains to the arrangements a distributor will need to put in place when distributing a new product, i.e. creating the relevant procedures and training to distribute the product in accordance with the instructions of the manufacturer, careful observation of the wording details that there is also an expectation to 'review distribution arrangements'. This is underlined by PRIN 2A.3.19R:

> "(1) A *distributor* must regularly review its distribution arrangements to ensure that they are still appropriate and up to date.
>
> (2) When reviewing the *distribution* arrangements, a distributor must verify that it is only *distributing* each *product* to the identified *target market.*"

Whilst there is no requirement for distributors to complete their own product reviews as such, there is an expectation that they take responsibility to review the success of their distribution arrangements in reaching the target market and providing support to reduce foreseeable harms and their support of customers to pursue their financial objectives. On a practical level it may be difficult for distributors to evaluate their success in the same way that manufacturers can, for the simple reason that they may not have access to information about the outcomes received by customers. A credit broker, for example, will take care to advertise the credit option in a fair, balanced and not misleading way and to meet the information needs of the customer throughout the sales journey. They may also assess the customer's objectives and suitability, using creditworthiness assessments to ascertain whether the product is appropriate. After this point, the customer is usually handed over to the lender for the final credit check and decision and often the broker will not hear anything more about the customer or their experience, unless the customer makes a complaint. The Duty encourages manufacturers to share more data with distributors, giving them data to enable an understanding of the outcomes received by customers; such data would enable a review of their distribution arrangements.

Manufacturers may, instead, choose to share the results of their product reviews. The reviews may contain valuable information and guidance for the distributor helping them to review their own distribution arrangements.

Certainly, as part of the review, distributors must ensure that they are receiving sufficient information from the manufacturer to enable them to distribute the product. At a minimum this information must enable the distributor to:

1. understand the characteristics of the product;
2. understand the identified target market;
3. consider the needs, characteristics and objectives of any retail customers in the target market with characteristics of vulnerability;
4. identify the intended distribution strategy for the product; and
5. ensure the product will be distributed in accordance with the needs, characteristics and objectives of the target market.

(PRIN 2A.3.16R)

Equally distributors must provide information to manufacturers upon request. The information may be used to support reviews undertaken by the manufacturer and could therefore include information about the distribution strategy, sales data and information about the reviews undertaken of the distribution strategy.

Where inconsistencies with the cross-cutting rules are identified by distributors, they are required to amend the distribution strategy to avoid the harm from continuing or occurring again in the future and to inform the manufacturer – as well as other firms in the distribution chain (where appropriate) – of the identified issue.

7.7: Groups of Customers

A technique which can be used by both manufacturers and distributors when conducting their reviews is to use data to analyse groups of customers, identifying whether they are achieving different outcomes and then taking steps to address the causes of the variation in outcomes.

The first step is to *categorise* groups of customers. Whilst this is wholly dependent on the type of product offered, there are some groups which are likely to be common to a wide array of products. Customers may be grouped by age, experience with financial services, level of education, income or vulnerability. Note with the last option it is imperative to split customers by type of vulnerability rather than one single 'vulnerable customer group'. This is because vulnerability, and its effects, are too wide to be covered within one group.

Firms may also use non-customer centric groupings, such as by distributor or the distribution channel that the customer was on-boarded with.

Once categorised, the objectives of the customers can be plotted – easier for non-advised products – and an analysis performed to understand whether the customer achieved the outcome they had in mind when they purchased the product. A customer purchasing a pension product may have aimed for a certain retirement income, their financial advisor working out the contributions needed by them and their family to achieve this goal. Perhaps this customer is part of the group of customers who did not have much experience with financial services. Their outcome can be reviewed (or if they have not reached retirement age yet the firm may choose to identify whether they are on course to achieve their aims) and taken together with a range of customers in this segment, can provide data detailing outcome success rates. This group may be compared to other groups, such as sophisticated investors or more / less wealthy customers. If their outcomes are different, it would indicate a weakness in the distribution of the product, perhaps it is not appropriate for a certain customer type or the information provided means customers are not selecting the best product for them. Once identified, this can then be addressed.

The comparative approach is particularly useful when analysing the outcomes of vulnerable customers. One group of vulnerable customers that may be focused on are customers with anxiety. An insurance provider may analyse the outcomes for customers with anxiety and identify a far greater number of customers not making claims. A root cause analysis may identify that many customers are maintaining cover they no longer need or did not need in the first place. As a result, the provider would put additional checks in the sales journey to identify whether the cover is required and may introduce correspondence, at regular intervals, to ask customers whether anything has changed. This correspondence would, of course, be written in a way that reassures the customer that they have the option to cancel, without reprisal, should they no longer require it.

7.8: Required Actions

The FCA requires that an organisation undertaking a product approval, or a product review, has a clear plan of action following the review. This must be recorded and demonstratable to the regulator should it be requested. Anecdotally, the author has seen action plans being requested by the FCA when tackling concerns about a product.

The action plan is the main output from the product review. It should detail negative findings, in other words, where the product or the way that it is distributed could cause harm to customers, or result in difficulty for customers when trying to pursue their financial objectives or where there are examples of poor faith in the product design. It should then detail the required solutions, or steps to be taken to address the issue together with a timescale and responsible individual. The regulator will want to see this plan communicated to senior management, evidence of careful consideration and management holding the responsible managers to account for completing their actions. As a result, it is also beneficial to identify an accountable individual for each action within the plan, this individual is to be charged with ensuring the timely completion of actions.

Communication plans should be part of the action plan, detailing what and who needs to be informed of the product weaknesses. Consideration should be given as to whether distributors, co-manufacturers and the regulator are to be informed with reasons for the decision made recoded.

Actions to be undertaken following assessment

Clear rules are set out, not only in relation to undertaking the assessment but also in relation to taking action following its completion. This applies to the reviews completed as part of the implementation plan as well as any subsequent reviews. Where the manufacturer has identified that the product or service may harm the customer, measuring against the cross-cutting rules, they must take steps to mitigate the situation and prevent further harms. Where the product has not yet been brought to market, the manufacturer is banned from releasing it until the harms have been addressed. It is equally as important to inform other firms in the distribution chain to enable them to take the appropriate action, usually amending the distribution strategy. This requirement is set out in PRIN 2A.3.8R and 2A.3.10R.

Equally, distributors are required to amend their distribution strategy to avoid identified harms from continuing and to inform the manufacturer as well as other firms in the distribution chain (where appropriate) of the identified issue.

Firms should also be mindful of the requirements under Principle 11, to be open and honest with the regulator and inform them of information they ought to be made aware of. Where the product review identifies significant failures, specifically where there is widespread customer detriment, the FCA must be made aware. Other factors which should be taken into account when deciding whether to inform the regulator include:

- whether the issue is likely to impact customers of other firms regulated by the FCA.
- if there is the risk of a systemic issue.
- where customer detriment is severe.
- where another firm in the distribution chain refuses to engage in information sharing, addressing the issue or any of its other obligations under the Duty.

CHAPTER EIGHT

PRODUCT REVIEWS: CLOSED MANUFACTURERS

8.1: Introduction

A closed product is defined in the FCA Handbook as a product:

(1) where there are existing contracts with retail customers entered into before 31 July 2023; and

(2) which is not marketed or distributed to retail customers (including by way of renewal) on or after 31 July 2023.

In short, it is a product which is no longer sold (as of August 2023) and cannot be renewed but still has a number of customers. An example is a mortgage product marketed and sold until 2020. The average customer may remain with the product for 25 years with some remaining for 35 years. This product is a closed product as it is no longer marketed and sold but still has customers remaining with it.

The Duty requires manufacturers to consider the needs of customers of closed products in much the same way as it does those entering, or remaining with, open products. Remember that the Duty requires a focus beyond the sale of the product to the entire experience of the customer.

8.2: Timing and Triggers

The obligation to conduct product reviews rests with the manufacturer. PRIN 2A.3.5R sets out the timing requirement: "A manufacturer of a closed product must maintain, operate and review a process to assess and regularly review whether any aspect of the product results in the firm not complying with the cross-cutting obligations in relation to existing retail customers". As with open product reviews there is little more to guide manufacturers as to the timing of the reviews. As such, one approach is to accept that timing is not, therefore, the primary catalyst of the review, instead it is events that could materially affect the potential risk to the customers. Manufacturers may build a series of key risk indicators (KRIs) to alert them that a review is required. The KRIs should focus on both internal and external factors which may harm customers. Examples include:

- Internal: Changes in customer behaviour, such as increase in default rates, switching or cancellation. Changes in contact rates from customers may indicate an issue with the product, as could a rise in complaints. Furthermore, identification of conflicts of interest, notification of problems by a distributor, customer journey reviews, use of the product itself, and monitoring use of online tracking or customer feedback can also indicate potential problems.

- External: Economic deviations can, of course, impact the relationship between the customer and the product, creating new harms through no fault of either party. Cost of living increases, or high rates of unemployment can place pressure on customer finances not previously foreseen by the manufacturer. Where firms are able to quantify such economic data into potential impact on their customer base, a useful KRI can be produced. Another example is that policy changes, such as increases in the base rate, may impact the product, e.g. customers of a closed mortgage product where the interest rate is not fixed. Other external factors could include technological changes meaning customers could achieve better results elsewhere, or changes in law impacting the product.

Another approach, often used where the KRI method is not appropriate, is to create an arbitrary timescale, usually annual or bi-annual.

Implementation of the Duty

Closed product reviews also have a place in the implementation of the Duty; manufacturers were given roughly one year to complete their open product reviews and take remedial action. An additional year was given to complete closed product reviews, therefore the first needed to have been completed by 31 July 2024.

8.3: Content

PRIN 2A.3.5R states:

> *"A manufacturer of a closed product must maintain, operate and review a process to assess and regularly review whether any aspect of the product results in the firm not complying with the cross-cutting obligations (*PRIN 2A.2*) in relation to existing retail customers."*

This is the overarching requirement and therefore the content of closed product reviews does not significantly differ from the open product review. However, there are certain exclusions, including:

- The requirement to approve closed products, which is a logical step as such products could no longer be created.
- The requirement to review the product's performance in relation to the distribution strategy, identifying if there are events which could materially impact the needs of the target market to which the product is distributed.
- The selection of distribution channels and information provided to distributors.
- The testing requirement.

The review will therefore need to set out the product features, including the intended benefits, natural limitations and risks. The impact the product has had on customers is central to the assessment and to this end an analysis of the use of the product is a helpful measure, especially when usage is viewed through the lens of different groups, or segments, of customers.

PRIN 2A.3.6R demonstrates one method is to assess whether the product impacts groups of customers in different ways, including whether vulnerable customers are affected differently. Therefore, manufacturers may segment their customer base by their characteristics, time with the product, vulnerability or distribution channel used to access the product in order to identify whether groups of customers receive different outcomes.

Characteristics which can be used to segment the customer base include financial experience, literacy, age, income or other demographics appropriate to the specific product or service.

Furthermore, the closed product review can assess compliance against the cross-cutting rules. It can identify if there is a lack of good faith through any undue friction, manipulation or exploitation of customers. An example might include behavioural biases present in the service, such as the website or online systems pushing customers towards a certain contact method because it is beneficial for the firm rather than meeting the customer's needs or preferences. A range of management information can contribute towards understanding whether the firm continues to act in good faith, including customer focus groups, customer feedback, customer query analysis, quality assurance results, complaints, customer journey audit, and up-to-date research on customer behaviour and/or vulnerable customers.

In respect of enabling and supporting customers to pursue their financial objectives, manufacturers may wish to review how they have identified their customer's objectives and ultimately supported customers towards achieving those objectives. An analysis of *how* the products have been *designed* to support customer objectives and whether this has been achieved is essential practice. Collating and examining data in relation to customers exiting or switching is valuable information to support this analysis.

The most extensive section is likely to be a review against the harms that customers may, foreseeably, face. The following questions may be asked:

1. Has the potential for harm where the product is withdrawn or changed been identified?

2. Are emerging trends that could identify new sources of harm regularly reviewed?

3. Has appropriate action to mitigate the risk of harm been taken where necessary?

4. Does awareness of and reaction to foreseeable harm happen throughout the lifecycle of the product?

5. Have inherent risks been identified?

6. Is there good evidence that the customers have accepted that risk?

7. How are inherent risks differentiated from foreseeable harm?

It is likely that firms will already capture much of the data required to enable the above questions to be answered. Information from quality assurance, customer journey audits, breaches and incidents, customer feedback, customer query analysis, communication reviews, themed reviews and complaints can provide rich data.

The four outcomes can then be considered. The review itself is meeting the obligations under the products and services outcome, so focus can instead be on price and value, consumer communication and consumer support.

Fair Value should be considered for closed products; does product design ensure that customer lack of knowledge and behavioural biases are not exploited for prices? Are pricing and terms clear and fair enabling customers to assess value? How does the cost of the product reflect value – are the benefits in line with the price? Where there have been, or are proposed, any changes to the product, will there be an accompanying reduction in price if a review highlights a reduction in benefits? Are accrued costs and benefits taken into account?

It is important to remember that the Duty has changed the standard required of communication from "clear, fair and not misleading" to "understandable for the target market", a wholly different standard which requires a subjective test which was not needed for the 'clear, fair and not misleading' standard. To be able to undertake such an assessment, it is imperative that the target market for the product is identified and their characteristics drawn out. Without doing so it is impossible to assess their information needs. Once those needs are identified, manufacturers can then check whether the communication methods and messages actually used meet the communication needs of customers both in terms of content and frequency. Again, it is recommended to consider vulnerable customers and their specific information needs separately.

The customer service provision must also be reviewed. The goal is to identify whether the service provided is congruent with the needs of the target market. The following questions can assist in ascertaining this point: Are the key product / service features being used as expected? Are they therefore meeting the needs of the customer base? Have customers been able to get the support they have needed in a timely and effective manner? Has appropriate friction enabled customers to make informed decisions about their use / cancellation of the product?

A range of useful management information may already be available to inform this review, such as call and email waiting times, call abandoned rates, switching take-up rates, complaints data, default rates, cancellation data, persistency / retention data and use of different add-ons.

Once complete, weak points should be obvious and therefore the foreseeable harms to customers made clear.

Form of assessment

There is no prescribed format of the assessment, as long as it covers the content stated above and meets the record keeping requirements as set out in SYSC. The assessment must also ensure that the effect the product has on groups of retail customers are reviewed (PRIN 2A.3.6), including vulnerable customers, therefore the format of the assessment must factor in this requirement.

8.4: Identifying poor faith

The steps that can be taken to identify a lack of good faith are the same for closed product reviews as they are for open product reviews. As outlined in the open product review section, the design of the product should be analysed, identifying whether the product exploits customers in any way. This can be supported by a review of the core-culture of the organisation, specifically looking for conflicts of interest which could give rise to actions that represent poor faith, remuneration arrangements and reward structures which, by their nature, encourage staff to measure their own performance in a way that does not promote good customer outcomes.

Closed products are, almost by definition, older than open products. This may lead some organisations to fear punishment where the design of the product does not meet the new standards of the Duty, or firms may require clarity to help them understand just how far they need to go to redesign the product or service. The Duty does not apply retrospectively, therefore where products or services were not compliant prior to implementation, no action will or can be taken by the regulator. As the implementation date for closed products was 31 July 2024, firms do not need to be concerned with the performance of the service prior to this date – save for where other regulations require them to do so. However, compliance is required after this date because where the product does not meet the standards required by the Duty, regulatory action can be taken. In other words, all products currently used by customers must comply with the Duty. The implementation period provided an important opportunity to review the performance and design of the product against the standards of the Duty, ensuring aspects that did not meet the standards were amended prior to the end of July 2024.

Older products are more likely to have characteristics of bad faith baked into them due to the fact products created more recently are likely to have been designed with the consumer Duty in mind or, at least, will be reflective of the customer-first culture which has been progressing over time. It is therefore imperative that manufacturers study the detail of closed products, drawing out instances where behavioural bias is relied upon to the customer's detriment, processes which have been intentionally designed to be difficult for customers to navigate (such as making a claim or raising a query), asking for evidence from customers where this is not justified, complex products which hide costs or risks or failing to contact customers prior to an event, such as going over an agreed overdraft which creates a cost for customers. In the final example, reaching out to customers to warn them in advance is an example of putting the customer's needs over the income to the firm and is therefore good faith.

Additionally, the following may be identifiers of poor faith:

- Products designed without proper testing. In the context of closed reviews, testing is not in relation to the sale of the product but post-sale support and communications. Communications are important to elicit the required response from customers and because the testing requirement is unlikely to have been present when a closed product was created, this is likely to be needed to be remediated for most closed products.

- Products designed without consideration of fair value, therefore the closed product review should be conducted alongside a fresh value assessment.
- A failure to act on recurring problems in the delivery of customer service.
- Failure to take action where it has been identified that harm is occurring.

To ascertain whether the product has been designed in poor faith, the manufacturer can utilise several pieces of MI, such as business persistence data that indicates a problem with the product. For example, a large percentage of customers switching or cancelling; analysis may point to a lack of good faith as the root cause. This could be due to several factors, one of which is the selection of an inappropriate target market, one that could be more likely to purchase the product, but that product may not be suitable for them. Whilst this is primarily a distribution issue, which would no longer apply to closed products, the existing customer base should be reviewed and where it is clear that the product is not benefiting the customer they should be informed and, where possible, moved to a more suitable product.

Other useful data may include complaints data, customer feedback, quality monitoring results or customer insights data which may indicate the customer 'drops off' the website at a certain point, indicative of the inclusion of inappropriate friction.

When reviewing MI, an effort should be made to look through a 'vulnerable customer lens', focusing on whether support provided, such as customer service and the quality of communications, is sufficient to enable vulnerable customers to achieve similar outcomes compared to customers who are not vulnerable. The starting point is to understand the objectives of customers who purchase the product, whether advised or not, and work back from this point, using MI, to ascertain whether customers have achieved these outcomes. Separating the findings by vulnerable and non-vulnerable customers will enable a direct comparison of outcomes. Where a difference is identified a root cause analysis will be able to highlight the reason for the difference, where it is due to a lack of faith, such as prioritising income over timely communications designed to warn customers, amendments must then be made.

8.5: Identifying foreseeable harms

Foreseeable harms can occur throughout the customer journey, from the receipt of the financial promotions, through the sales process until the end of the relationship. It is the latter element that is to be focused on when identifying harm in relation to closed products. The scope of the review is therefore limited to the provision of customer service (post-sale) and communications issued to the customer.

Broadly, three categories of harms can apply to closed products. Firstly, poor support in relation to a change in circumstances. The change may derive from an alteration in the customer's situation or from broader economic factors. An example is a customer falling into financial difficulties, perhaps due to job loss, which could impact their ability to repay a mortgage or loan product. Other examples include variations in the rate of interest due to be paid, perhaps due to a base rate change, resulting in a previously affordable product becoming unaffordable. Such harms are foreseeable and therefore must be identified during the product review. Mitigation is clearly through the relevant communication and support allowing the customer flexible options to help reduce the harm. In the example of the mortgage which has started to attract a higher interest rate, enabling the customer to switch to a more affordable product, take a break in payments, or temporarily pay a reduced amount would all be appropriate solutions.

Another example to highlight this point is in relation to insurance cover where, due to a change in the customer's circumstances, they no longer require the level of cover they previously purchased. Again, communicating the options available to customers in this situation and providing product flexibility, such as moving to a more appropriate insurance product, is the standard expected.

Secondly, communication, or lack of it, can be a source of harm. A focus of closed reviews must be whether communications are as effective as they could be in order to enable customers to make effective decisions. Because the standard of communication has been changed from the need to be "clear, fair and not misleading" to "understandable for the target market" there are almost certainly improvements which can be made in light of the new standard. Therefore, as manufacturers assess the characteristics of customers who have purchased the product, they must also take steps to understand and meet their information needs.

Finally, the provision of good quality customer services is central to avoiding harm in relation to closed products. Customer service clearly does not stop at the point of sale as customers require support, perhaps due to the circumstance changes we have already outlined in this section, the response of the firm will either cause harm or actively take steps to avoid harm. This applies to customer queries, complaints and disputes that may be raised from time to time. Data such as first point of contact resolution figures, complaint root causes and quality monitoring of responses can be used to help ascertain the quality of customer support provided.

Despite the temptation to put distributors aside when we consider closed products, manufacturers must remember they may well impact the customers' experience, particularly where the role of the distributor is not purely sales but includes an ongoing relationship with the customer as is often the case with services such as financial advice. The selection process of distributors, ensuring they have the relevant skills, processes and resources in place to provide the level of ongoing support needed can therefore be included in the review. Where harms are the fault of the service provided by the distributor, the manufacturer is under a duty to ensure the provider changes their approach or the manufacturer changes provider.

8.6: Identifying poor financial outcomes

Enabling and supporting customers to pursue their financial objectives is a central pillar of the Duty and therefore must be considered in product reviews. Taking the actions to avoid foreseeable harm and act in good faith go much of the way towards meeting this cross-cutting rule. For example, it was highlighted that customers who experience a change in financial circumstances (financial difficulty) should be provided good levels of customer support, through product flexibility, to avoid or mitigate the harm that arises from financial difficulties. This support will also help the customer to pursue their financial objectives through being able to continue to use the product. Incidentally, taking action such as allowing lower than contractual payments for a period of time is also an example of acting in good faith.

Whilst there is clearly a lot of cross over between the three cross-cutting rules, a standalone section in the closed product review will enable the manufacturer to identify instances where customers' financial objectives are not supported and where this has not been captured in other areas of the review. Examples may include the identification of overly flexible commission structures – enabling distributors to levy charges to the extent they no longer provide good value, or where the price of the product has moved significantly beyond the original expectation and as such no longer provides good value to customers. Both examples focus on value, which is only natural when exploring financial objectives, however the review should also take into account the design of the product, communication, and support as each in turn may also affect the ability of customers to pursue their objectives.

8.7: Distributors

Some distributors may continue to have a relationship with customers following the sale of the product or service, where this is the case, they will fall into the scope of closed product reviews. It is then logical that instructions will flow from the review to the distributor requiring them to take identified actions to avoid harm, a lack of faith in the delivery of the service, and to help customers to meet their objectives.

It is natural for distributors to want to commit as little resources as possible into managing accounts post-sale, except where there is the possibility or aim to obtain repeat custom. However, this attitude must be seen as a risk, not only to compliance with the Duty but also to the outcomes that customers receive. It directly contradicts the cultural change driven by the Duty. Instead, distributors must be aware of the need to move past the 'money-first' culture to a 'customer-first' culture where the ongoing needs of customers are central to the product or service design, even where this attracts greater costs for the distributor.

Manufacturers have the responsibility to review the outcomes of customers on closed products and where they identify a problem, including where the problem is due to the actions of a distributor or where it is only a distributor who can remedy the problem, they are required to set remedial actions. As a result, distributors will be told the steps that must be completed. The requirement from a distributor's point of view is to understand and follow those instructions.

8.8: Groups of Customers

As with open product reviews, a useful technique is to use data to analyse groups of customers, identifying whether they are achieving different outcomes and then taking steps to address the causes of the variation in outcomes.

Again, the first step is to categorise groups of customers, this may include age, experience with financial services, level of education, income or type of vulnerability. Segmentation focused on different areas than customer characteristics can also be useful, such as the distribution channel the customer used to purchase the product, as this may have an impact on their understanding of the closed product, and they may require additional information to help ensure consistency between customers.

Analysis can then be conducted to determine whether customers, based on their segment, receive similar outcomes to other customers. Where a group of customers appear to receive worse outcomes, steps must be taken to remedy the situation.

8.9: Addressing gaps

Actions to be taken following assessment

PRIN 2A.3.8R requires manufacturers to take action to mitigate identified harms and prevent further harm. This is required following closed product reviews, as it is with open reviews. It is also important that other firms in the distribution chain, where they could impact the customer, are notified of any actions to be taken to mitigate the risk of harm.

Save for situations where the distributor has an ongoing relationship with the customer, the majority of steps taken to address gaps will be in relation to customer service support and communications to help customers understand harms or where they are not getting as much from the product as they could and to take steps to avoid potential harms or get more from their product. It is easy to see how customers would feel more confident and become more trusting with their financial products where this is actioned correctly.

CHAPTER NINE

CONSUMER UNDERSTANDING OUTCOME

9.1: Overview

Consumers are unlikely to be able to get the most from financial products unless they understand the product. In order to achieve this aim, the consumer Duty is focused on improving the level and sophistication of communication received by customers.

The regulator's intention can be best summarised by the following quote "Consumers can only be expected to take responsibility where firms' communications enable them to understand their products and services, their features and risks, and the implications of any decisions they must make" (FG 22/5, p.71). In this section of the final guidance the FCA confirms the following as their primary objectives from this outcome:

- customers will be supported to make informed decisions
- information is provided in a timely manner
- firms consider which communication channel is most appropriate
- communications are tested
- customers will be provided with the information they need, at the right time, and in a way they can understand (tailored communication).

The final aim listed above, ensuring that information is presented in a way that customers can understand, is outlined in PRIN 2A.5.4R which requires the same for product specific communications. The standard is a step-change from the previous communication requirement. As already stated in this book, the consumer Duty principle (principle 12 under PRIN 2) replaces principle 6 (a firm must pay due regard to the interests of its customers and treat them fairly) and principle 7 (a firm must pay due regard to the information needs of its clients and communicate information to them in a way which is clear, fair and not misleading). The new standard is significantly different from the principle 7 standard which was an objective criterion, asking whether, to the average person, was the communication of the firm clear, fair and not misleading? There was no expectation to tailor communication to the needs of the customer or consider the context in which the communication was delivered. Under the Duty, the requirement to provide information "in a way [the customer] can understand" is subjective in its nature, considering the information needs of the customer.

To apply the subjective methodology those creating communications should consider the characteristics of customers in the intended target market for the product, or in the case of closed products the characteristics of the customers who have already purchased the product. The characteristics can be used to identify the likely information needs of the target market, for example, where the target market is predominantly customers with poor experience with financial services it is logical that they might require the basic aspects of the product to be explained to them. Additionally, the target market's characteristics can inform the method and timing of communication, such as communications provided in 'bite-sized' stages to enable easier consumption of the key points. This approach is particularly useful where decisions need to be made by the customer as the pertinent pieces of information can be timed to coincide with the point in time where the decision is required. Again, the requirements in PRIN 2A support this thinking with PRIN 2A.5.6R requiring:

> *"In considering the methods of communicating with retail customers, a firm must satisfy itself that the communication channel:*
>
> *a) enables the communication of relevant information which retail customers are likely to need in a way that supports effective decision making; and*
>
> *b) provides an appropriate opportunity for retail customers to review the information and, where relevant, assess their options."*

Some consumers may prefer data supplied in electronic form, others in written format, or even verbal. There may be certain points in time where electronic notification may be more useful and others where a written letter will have a greater impact. When designing products, manufacturers should design their communication strategies in accordance with these preferences.

The previous clear, fair and not misleading rule does still apply as a base minimum, but it is built upon by the new subjective requirement as highlighted by the FCA in their final guidance:

> *"Our consumer understanding outcome rules retain the obligation under Principle 7 for firms to communicate information in a way which is clear, fair and not misleading. But they also build on, and go further than, Principle 7 by requiring firms to:*
>
> - *support their customers' understanding by ensuring that their communications meet the information needs of customers, are likely to be understood by customers intended to receive the communication, and equip them to make decisions that are effective, timely and properly informed*

- *tailor communications taking into account the characteristics of the customers intended to receive the communication – including any characteristics of vulnerability, the complexity of products, the communication channel used, and the role of the firm*

- *when interacting directly with a customer on a one-to-one basis, where appropriate, tailor communications to meet the information needs of the customer, and ask them if they understand the information and have any further questions*

- *test, monitor and adapt communications to support understanding and good outcomes for customers"*

(FG 22/5, p.71)

9.2: Scope

The communication requirements apply to all firms involved in approving, distributing and producing customer communications whether the firm has a direct relationship with the customer or not. It also applies at all stages of the customer journey, from financial promotions through to product realisation.

The medium of the communication does not matter as the requirements apply to verbal, written and electronic communications.

9.3: Principles of good customer communication:

There are principles of good communication which can be applied across a range of situations, these are designed to enhance the clarity of communications and support customers to make better, informed decisions.

Layering

Layering has historically been used to the detriment of customers. It involves setting out key points of information in the first document the customer encounters (often the first page of a letter, main body of an email or first webpage) with further information gained by clicking on links within that initial document (where online) or reading documents referred to in the front page of the letter. The FCA's research in the Asset Management Market Study demonstrated that customers are less likely to read information that they have to seek out, it is therefore easy to see why hiding charges, product limitations or other such key information would, in many cases, lead to customers purchasing a product which will not function in the way that they expected and, in the worst cases, may be unsuitable. Where layering has been used to disguise information about charges or fees or make undesirable information less prominent it would be an example of poor faith as well as failing to meet the FCA's expectations in relation to this outcome.

On the other hand, layering can be used to support effective communication, particularly where a lot of information needs to be conveyed. Effective layering involves highlighting the key, important points, in the first document in a way which is balanced (fairly representing the customer's interests and the firm's). The skill is to properly identify what the key / important points are and to do so the creator needs to be able to put themselves in the customer's shoes, using the subjective test to include information that customers from the target market are likely to require. There are obvious pieces of information to always include, such as information in relation to cost, charges and product risks.

Engaging

Thought needs to be given as to how to design communication so that it is engaging for customers. The FCA's final guidance (FG 22/5) highlights the importance of doing so where the communication is intended to prompt the customer to take action.

Communications can be made to be engaging through headings and use of boxes to draw attention to the most important messages, such as those requiring the customer to act. Attempts at this have been made in the past, for example the Consumer Credit Act 1974 requires (at the time of writing) certain information in default notices to be capitalised to draw the customer's attention to the risks of defaulting on their credit agreement, however this style of wording is now perceived as aggressive and therefore not customer friendly. Reflecting on this example tells us that careful thought must be given to achieve a balance between drawing the attention of customers towards key information and presenting that information in a way which is not perceived as aggressive. Incidentally, the FCA has confirmed that where a statutory requirement, such as the Consumer Credit Act 1974 example, requires wording to be presented in a certain way, even where this is incompatible with the Duty, firms should continue to comply with the statutory requirement.

The best communications use visual graphics where it is possible to do so; tables, charts and infographics can be immensely effective at presenting complex information in a concise, readable way which is more likely to be read and absorbed by recipients. According to the FCA's research by their behavioural insights team, terms and conditions presented in a question-and-answer format can increase engagement by up to 36%.

Relevant

We've all been on the receiving end of 'over-communication', whether in the form of contracts, terms and conditions or even key information documents. It is where the customer is provided with so much information that it becomes overbearing, resulting in poorer engagement. Such communication has often been an area of criticism for the regulator, as their demands to "deliver information to customers" is most often the root cause. Nevertheless, firms have been guilty as well, some using over-communication to draw attention away from certain aspects of the product where others, acting in good faith, have over-interpreted regulatory requirements. The FCA have warned firms against doing so; more information does not always equate to more compliance.

Instead, firms should look to ensure that the information selected to be included in communication is relevant to the situation. This includes appreciating the nature of the product. Low risk products clearly do not require the same amount of information as those which pose a risk to customers. Firms should avoid needlessly overloading customers or including, for example, unnecessary disclaimers.

Actions that can assist with achieving this principle include breaking down communications; the bite-sized approach improves the relevancy of information where it is delivered at the right time. Using simpler wording and explaining complicated terms can increase comprehension.

Simple

One of the most difficult skills of communication is appreciating that the individual receiving the communication does not have the knowledge the sender has. This is true when communicating on an individual level or at an organisational level. Typically, the individuals who design, review and sign-off customer communications are industry experts, those who have worked in financial services for many years. It's therefore difficult for them to recognise where technical information is included, such as phrases referring customers to certain organisations within the industry, or where terms are stated which may not be interpreted in the same way by the customer.

The goal is to 'strip-back' communications, avoiding jargon, terms only likely to be properly understood by those within the industry or those by individuals with higher reading ages. The latter point is particularly important where the product is designed for customers who are less likely to have high levels of education.

To achieve the goal an additional layer within the organisation's communication review and sign-off process is required, one where lay individuals are consulted so that it can be truly understood how customers are likely to interpret information.

Well timed

Timing is everything. This is best described by the FCA in FG 22/5, p.75 "Firms should communicate with customers in a timely manner and at appropriate touch points throughout the product lifecycle, such as at contractual breakpoints, giving them an appropriate opportunity to take in the information and, where relevant, assess their options. This will help to put customers in a position where they can make effective decisions on an informed basis".

9.4: Tailoring Communications

Historically a 'one size fits all' approach has been sufficient, however FCA expectations have clearly shifted. Organisations are now required to properly understand their target market and design communications to meet their information needs. The expectations are best portrayed through the following example:

> A financial services firm launches a finance app, designed to provide a range of ISAs designed for 18–35-year-olds such as a lifetime ISA, longer-term investment ISAs and easy access cash ISAs. They recognise their customer base is likely to have a mix of needs, such as saving for a first home, retirement planning and is likely to need to gain access to some or all of their savings at some point in the future.
>
> They design the App to provide their customers with information, in small chunks, while they investigate the products or sign-up to them. This information clearly presents how each ISA product works, setting out clear and relevant information such as costs related to withdrawals. It also guides the customer through the rules in relation to

opening ISAs, such as the limitation on how many they can open in a tax-year.

The content is simplified, with the above selected information provided to support their decision making, a single click provides explanations on key terms such as explaining what an ISA is. The firm then presents the customer with a small number of questions to answer, designed to understand their financial goals and position, factored into a simple decision tree which may, by way of an example, suggest that a proportion of the customer's savings are invested in an easy access ISA, another lump to a lifetime ISA, and once those products have been maximised, a stocks and shares ISA.

When customers are able to open a second ISA, they are provided with a notification on their phone informing them that this is now possible. The steps taken are a prime example of the information needs of customers being taken into account as well as the delivery of that information through electronic notifications, clearly the most suitable way to engage with the target market.

In this example the communication has been tailored by taking into account all of the principles of good customer communications.

9.5: Interaction with statutory or regulatory notices

Whilst there are statutory and regulatory notices which are not entirely compatible with the Duty, the majority of them have been designed to provide customers with certain information to help customers make effective decisions. Because of this and the fact the Duty does not, and is not capable of, amending statutory requirements, they should be complied with.

Of course, some regulatory notices have an element of discretion built into them to enable firms to select the most relevant information for customers. Where this is the case, firms should follow the same principles as they would for any other communication under the Duty.

Nevertheless, where statutory information is required, firms are still encouraged to think of the information requirements of the customer and assess whether the information, in the required form, will meet those information needs. Where possible, additional information, in the form of cover letters, links or extra paragraphs, will aid the customer's understanding of the statutory information and should be provided to the customer.

The following helpful examples are set out in the final guidance:

> *Example – poor practice*
>
> *A firm provides a product sales pack to a customer, including cover letter, summary sheet, and full terms and conditions. The cover letter explains the cost of the product during an introductory offer period; the summary sheet explains the cost of the product at the end of the offer period; and the full terms and conditions explain the costs of cancelling the product. This information is not clearly signposted. The customer therefore needs to read and digest all three documents to find and understand the total costs associated with the product. This makes it difficult for the customer to identify and understand key information needed to make an effective decision. Firms should help consumers navigate the information they provide. For example, by putting all information on a particular issue in one place or signpost or layer it in a way so it is all interlinked.*
>
> (FG 22/5, p.76)

Example – poor practice

An insurance product has been updated over the course of several years, but the documents for this product have not been reviewed as a whole to make sure they continue to explain the product's features in a way that supports consumer understanding. The policy summary sets out upfront what is covered by the insurance and some specific exclusions to this cover. However, some newer, but equally important, exclusions are covered elsewhere in the full policy conditions. This makes it difficult for customers to assess the scope of the insurance and understand when they will, and will not, be covered.

(FG 22/5, p.76)

Example – good practice

The summary box for savings accounts in our Banking Conduct of Business (BCOBS) rules requires firms to state the rates of interest that apply and provide 'an explanation of the circumstances in which each of the different rates applies.' A firm has a savings product where various rates of interest apply in different circumstances. The firm identifies through its testing activity that consumers in the target market for the product struggle to understand the various rates of interest and the different circumstances in which each rate would apply. The firm therefore simplifies its product, reducing the number of interest rates and conditions applicable to each rate. This enables consumers to more easily understand the product and make effective decisions.

(FG 22/5, p.77)

9.6: Testing and monitoring requirements

Testing: what

As we have explored, a difficulty when writing communications is to move beyond what the designers of the communications understand to create communications which are truly understood by those who are receiving them.

It is safe to assume that firms are unable to test all communications, therefore selection criteria are required. This is an appropriate policy as the requirements in PRIN 2A.5.10 only require firms to conduct testing "where appropriate".

Prioritisation should be given to communication designed to give information that will be used when making a decision (such as whether to purchase a product), where the communication impacts a lot of customers, where the inherent risk of the product is high, and if the recipients are likely to have characteristics of vulnerability, particularly if they have lower levels of financial resilience, expertise or understanding. Conversely if the communication is required urgently to reduce the risk or severity of harm then it may be provided without testing, even where testing would usually be expected.

In the round PRIN 2A.5 requirements go beyond written communication, for example PRIN 2A.5.9, covers one to one conversations as well as other interactive dialogue.

Testing: when

PRIN 2A.5.10R formally requires testing to be conducted before a communication is provided to customers.

Testing: who

Firms responsible for issuing the communication will generally be responsible for testing them, however it may be the case that the manufacturer chooses to take responsibility for all testing.

Monitoring

PRIN 2A.5.10R also requires the ongoing monitoring of the impact communications have on customers once they have been communicated. This is to identify whether they are supporting good customer outcomes. In other words, have they achieved what they were designed to?

Monitoring is the responsibility of the organisation having direct interactions with the customer, as realistically they will be the only body able to assess the impact.

PRIN 2A.510R also provides a short list of actions which must be taken should it become apparent that a communication is not supporting customer outcomes or whether there are common misunderstandings being shown by the monitoring. These include investigating the issue, resolving any deficiencies identified, and providing redress where harm is identified as a result. The remedial action will therefore usually involve amending the relevant communications and informing others in the distribution chain of the need to do so; however, it could also include adapting the product or service itself.

9.7: Example

A financial services firm creates a mass market investment product. As a product which is inherently low risk, it would not be expected to have the same level of oversight and testing of its communications as a higher risk product. Should the organisation bring a new investment product to the market, such as a complex, higher risk product, it would not be reasonable to lift and drop the communications from the mass market investment product. Instead, the firm must have built into its product approval process a point to assess the risk of the product and create, test and monitor communications appropriately.

The manufacturer must understand the intended target market, their level of sophistication, reading level, vulnerabilities prevalent in the market and what they are reasonably likely to know about the type of product, to design a communication strategy which is:

1. Engaging
2. Layered (where appropriate)
3. Relevant
4. Simple
5. Well-timed

The likely starting point is to consider how customers will engage with the product, whether sales are online, made digitally, face to face or via the telephone. Perhaps a range of these distribution channels are to be used.

Focusing on online sales, the process could be designed to highlight the key features, risks, benefits and limitations of the product on the page of the website advertising it. Wording is carefully selected to be understandable for the target markets reading age, with consumer sample testing used to refine the wording. Some phrases or words which were found to be difficult for customers to understand could be further explained by way of a link: simply clicking on the word provides a simple definition. To avoid over-communicating, information can be layered throughout the sales process, providing the right information at the point in time a decision is to be made.

Post-implementation testing should also occur, in order to identify common misunderstandings or where the information has not provoked the expected reaction.

CHAPTER TEN

CONSUMER SUPPORT OUTCOME

10.1: Overview of the requirement

It is important to remember that despite much of the emphasis being on the sales process, the Duty owed to consumers does not stop at the point of sale. Post sale support is just as important as pre-sale, in fact it is often the cause of serious consumer harm.

The consumer support outcome is intrinsically interlinked with the other aspects of the Duty, this is because "consumers can only pursue their financial objectives where firms support them in using products and services they have bought" (FG 22/5, p.92) and "A product or service that a customer cannot properly use and enjoy is unlikely to offer fair value (FG 22/5, p.92)". It's also easy to envisage how poor consumer support can lead to foreseeable harms occurring which may in turn result in a product or service failing to perform. The relationship with consumer understanding is best described by the FCA in their final guidance "There is a close relationship between the rules under the consumer support outcome and the consumer understanding outcome. Under the consumer understanding outcome firms should communicate with customers in a way that equips them to make effective, timely and properly informed decisions. Under the consumer support outcome firms should enable customers to act on these decisions without facing unreasonable barriers. Firms should keep their obligations under both outcomes at the front of mind in all their interactions with their customers." (FG 22/5, p.92). Furthermore, the cause of the poor support may well be a lack of good faith on the part of the manufacturer or distributor, perhaps due to a lack of willingness to invest appropriately in the provision of support.

Wealth management is an excellent example of the importance of ongoing consumer support. Typically, a wealth management organisation will work with financial advisors who are tasked with understanding the investors' financial objectives, financial circumstances and attitude to risk before providing them with investment advice. This advice must be designed to enable the investor to have the best opportunity to meet their financial objectives. This may include understanding whether they are able to absorb losses which may occur if the investments do not perform, and willing to take the risk that this may occur. Appropriate financial advice will also ascertain whether the investor is likely to need to withdraw money from the investment in the short, medium and long-term, and placing those funds into investments which enable access in line with the customer's potential needs. It is of paramount importance that the advice at this stage is correct and takes into account the customer's circumstances. The advice is central to the consumer support outcome.

The wealth management firm cannot neglect their customer support at this point, they must consider the needs of their customers on a forward-looking basis. It is reasonable to assume customers will want to track their investment performance from time to time, inform their advisor of a change in their circumstances, simply ask questions, or withdraw a portion of their investment. The service provision must be able to meet these reasonable expectations. Imagine the customer urgently needed to withdraw funds, perhaps due to a sudden financial emergency but the online portal failed to function correctly, the customer couldn't get hold of the advisor and the firm didn't respond to the customer's emails.

Another reason a customer may decide to withdraw funds could be due to a sudden down-turn in investment performance. For clarity, we are not suggesting this would be the best option in the case of a down-turn, instead the customer's reaction is simply for illustrative purposes. The customer may well have been notified of their investment performance by the firm directly, perhaps due to a policy where customers are notified when their investments lose a certain level of value, another example of good consumer support. This example serves to demonstrate why customer service is just as important after the point of sale as it is during.

In our wealth management example, the wealth management firm is likely to be the manufacturer. The advisor, if self-employed, would be the distributor. The outcome applies to all organisations, whether manufacturers or distributors, who "are responsible for interacting directly with, and providing support to, retail customers, such as through its customer services functions and including where the firm outsources its interactions with retail customers to a third party (in whole or part);" (PRIN 2A.6.1R).

The stage of the customer journey is irrelevant, simply put, all customer support falls within the scope of this outcome.

10.2: Tailoring support

Manufacturers and distributors must design and deliver their support to ensure that customers can use the products as they reasonably expect, vulnerable customers are appropriately supported, and unreasonable post-sale barriers are avoided where customers want to raise a query, submit a complaint, switch products, cancel or move to another provider. The design of the support must be tailored to the customer's needs, meaning customers must be able to utilise the support provided.

The concept at the core of the requirement to tailor support is that different customers have different needs, and, where possible, it is the responsibility of all firms in the distribution chain to identify those needs and design their aspect of the service around them. The starting point is to analyse the target market for the product. This should be helpfully set out in the manufacturer's product approval or review. Analysis of the target market is intended to enable an understanding of the characteristics of customers and therefore the support that may be required by them. To achieve this the following areas may be focused on:

A) Likely understanding of the product or service (through a review of the customers experience with financial services or similar products)

B) Ability to make a reasoned decision (focusing on experience, education, time-pressures or factors of vulnerability which may impair decision making)

C) Ability to use support functions (such as online portals, Apps, contact centres, etc)

D) Difficulty accessing a service (disability, cognitive impairment, time-pressure).

All of the areas above can be applied to post-sale support as well as to the sales process. Customers may need to maintain an understanding of the product throughout their journey with it. An insurance product, for example, will need to be understood by the customer at the outset in order to weigh up whether it is needed and the level of cover desired, but the customer will also need to maintain an understanding past this point in time in order to make a claim, update the provider with changes to their circumstances or submit a query. Furthermore, customers may need to maintain an understanding of their ability to switch to another provider, should a more appropriate option be identified at a later date.

The process to undertake is to firstly consider what the customer needs to be able to do with the product. As described above this is likely to include understanding, accessing, using and losing the product. Losing, in this context, means cancelling or switching. Secondly the difficulties (or barriers) faced by the target market should be mapped against the needs of the customer. Once mapped it should be obvious where customers require support, following this the specific support steps can be identified.

10.3: Support

Information provision is often the first consideration when building a suite of customer support options. Re-designing a firm's standard information from both a sales and non-sales perspective can be helpful to support an individual's understanding. However, this will only be effective where real effort has been made to truly understand the characteristics of customers in the target market, establishing the gaps in their understanding and filling those with timely communication. The problem faced by the customer may be that gap in understanding, but it may also be an inability to digest information when provided in the standard way. In which case, the solution is not to provide *more* information but to consider how the information is provided to the customer, perhaps breaking it down into smaller, digestible, chunks. Clearly information provided during on-boarding are candidates for such treatment, as are regular statements, updates, key event information or information about renewals.

Whilst written communications are important, it is imperative that other support options are focused on in a similar way. The call centre provision must also be tailored to the needs of the customer, specifically designed around the target market. This involves call centre agents being able to communicate with different customers in a way that is understandable for them, meaning that an enhanced programme of training has become the norm for front line staff to help them better understand their target market, likely differences in customer characteristics between different products the firm might offer, the issues those customers may face, relevant solutions, and how best to communicate those solutions. Where this level of training is achieved it is likely the firm will significantly improve outcomes for their customers.

The success of the call centre support provision is dependent on the ability of customers to access it. Waiting times, cut off rates and operational resilience factors such as down time should also be considered when designing customer support.

Support may also be in the form of complaints handling, dispute resolution or answering questions from customers. The latter is often a source of frustration for customers; it follows that it is a weaker area of customer support. Whilst implementing the Duty many firms recognised, through their product reviews, that they had poor first contact resolution rates. In other words, after customers raised a query and had received an answer they came back to ask again. Root cause analysis revealed the response to the first set of questions were of poor quality, largely down to three factors. Firstly, the responding agent failing to properly understand the customer's concerns or question, therefore providing a response which did not address the questions the customer had. Often the response would have little to do with the question; these types of responses can be very confusing for the customer. Second was a focus on the main issue asked about, meaning other questions raised were ignored, prompting the customer to ask again and giving the customer the impression that the initial response was rushed. Thirdly, answers which have not been constructed to be understandable for the customer, perhaps due to the complex language used or the lack of context given to explanations. Tackling these areas have enabled firms to improve their consumer support, remain compliant with the relevant outcome, and the enhanced responses better support customers to achieve fair value from their products as well as avoid harms.

Another form of customer support is positive friction, which can be built into the support provision in a way that supports good customer outcomes. This concept is clearer in relation to sales, friction can support customer decision making by slowing the decision-making process at the critical point in time, asking customers to consider all of the relevant information to decide whether the product is right for them. Post-sale friction is a more difficult concept. Such friction is usually associated with negative outcomes, such as preventing customers from reaching their preferred method of consumer support where this is more costly to the firm than other methods. Other examples include friction designed to prevent a customer from switching to a more appropriate product, cancelling or complaining.

Positive post-sale friction can, and should, be incorporated into the design of the product or service. Examples include:

- When renewing agreements, such as insurance cover, enabling customers to pause and check whether the product is still right for them.
- Prior to making a decision which could cause harm to them, such as withdrawing early from an investment product, particularly where there is a cost to the customer for doing so.
- Moving to a higher risk investment portfolio.
- When re-completing suitability assessments.
- Making a transaction which could, potentially, be the result of the customer falling victim to fraud.
- When considering whether another product is more appropriate, such as on the suggestion of the manufacturer following a review of their needs.

Support must also be tailored to assist and meet the needs of vulnerable customers.

10.4: Vulnerable customers

An ever-increasing area of focus is the support that vulnerable customers receive. The regulator's expectations in this area date back to their inception, with multiple sections of the FCA Handbook requiring firms to take the needs of vulnerable customers into account and Occasional Paper No.8 providing guidance on good and poor practices. However, more recently, additional focus has been brought by the FCA's Vulnerable Customer Guidance, released in February 2021.

Vulnerability is a consistent thread throughout almost all work the regulator undertakes, with guidance documents often having a dedicated 'vulnerability' section.

For example, in February 2024 the FCA communicated their review of firms' implementation of the Duty, providing examples of a range of good and poor practices. The third section of this review, nestled between consumer Duty stalwarts 'governance, culture and monitoring' and the 'products and services' outcome, is 'Consumers in vulnerable circumstances'. Similarly in May 2024, the FCA released a series of Dear CEO letters providing guidance on closed product reviews, again these letters had a section dedicated to vulnerable customers. It is almost as if vulnerability support has become a consumer Duty outcome of its own.

Products and services can be designed to avoid harm to vulnerable customers during the sales process, however the majority of interactions with the subject of vulnerability takes place in the post-sale customer service provision. It is therefore of utmost importance for the design of customer support.

Defining vulnerability

A vulnerable customer is defined by the Financial Conduct Authority as "someone who, due to their personal circumstances, is especially susceptible to harm, particularly when a firm is not acting with appropriate levels of care." (FG 21/1, p.3)

Whilst this is quite a broad definition, further guidance is provided to better equip firms to ascertain whether an individual is vulnerable or not. This guidance is in relation to the four drivers of vulnerability, which are:

1. Health
2. Life Events
3. Resilience

4. Capability

Most individuals working in financial services would naturally equate vulnerability to the first driver, health. Conditions such as depression, anxiety, Alzheimer's and other mental health conditions together with physical health conditions are included in this first pillar. Life events such as bereavement may also be something that most people would naturally understand to be something that could make a person vulnerable. Life events do, however, go beyond bereavement to include job loss, change in financial circumstances resulting in financial difficulties, or relationship break up.

Less commonly understood are the latter two, resilience and capability. A lack of resilience is an inability to withstand emotional or financial shock and capability is usually understood as low knowledge of financial matters, low confidence when dealing with financial matters as well as poor literacy or digital skills and low mental capacity.

A lack of resilience or capability will rarely present as an issue on its own, especially where products have been designed to the standard expected with the Duty but can play a role in adding to another vulnerability. For example, Customer A may have little experience with financial services and poor literacy skills meaning it is more difficult for him/her to understand product literature and therefore poor confidence when dealing with financial services. However, they manage to engage with Firm B to obtain a credit card which they needed to support their tight cash-flow. They have managed to understand the basic functionality of the card, are able to use it and make payments towards the balance each month. Perhaps Firm B identifies that the customer makes payments at an inconsistent rate, sometimes paying in full, other times only the minimum balance and others not even this amount. As a result, they reach out the Customer A to explain the impact of paying less than is required and offering support to pay consistently, perhaps through setting up a direct debit. Customer A then loses their job, resulting in financial difficulty because they no longer have sufficient income to meet their reasonable living expenses and bills as they fall due. Another customer may understand the need to contact Firm B to explain the situation and request a payment break while they found another job, Customer A however, due to their lack to understanding and experience may not appreciate the support which can be provided and may be scared the card will be taken off them. This is an example of low capability and resilience adding to another vulnerability to cause harm. Think of vulnerability like a spectrum where issues, once layered on top of each other, can push customers up the spectrum towards a threshold where harm occurs. It is the responsibility of Firm B, as well as all financial services firms to do everything they can to identify customers in such situations and step in to provide support.

Identifying vulnerabilities

Identification can be following disclosure, either from the customer or a third party (we will discuss the data protection considerations later on in this chapter), or from a range of other mechanisms that can be built by a firm. Customer insights data, for example, can be used to identify spending or behavioural patterns indicating vulnerability, such as the inconsistent spending in our earlier example, high expenditure to gambling companies or sudden increases in spending, especially where the customer is known to have a condition which could cause impulsive decisions. Where such patterns are identified, the customer support provision should be designed to reach out to the customer to investigate and offer support.

Customer facing staff must be able to identify vulnerability as it is the starting point for offering tailored support. From this point of view, vulnerability may be identified following outright disclosure, or they may identify risk factors during a conversation or following receipt of written communication. Customers failing to remember information that has already been provided to them, obviously failing to comprehend information, incoherent writing or speech, a clear inability to make a decision and appearing distracted are all factors which could indicate a level of vulnerability. Furthermore, the customer may not go as far as disclosing an issue, instead they simply allude to one, such as stating "I'm between jobs" or "I'm not very well at the moment". Once an indicator has been identified, the staff member may reach out to the customer to invite them to provide more information. Simply asking the customer whether they are ok can be an effective way to do so. Once the customer has been invited to tell them more about their situation, then the onus is on the customer to do that to allow staff to assess which support options will be most suitable for their circumstances. If the customer declines to say more, then staff and the firm have given the customer the opportunity to discuss their circumstances.

Recording vulnerabilities

All too often Data Protection is cited as a barrier to providing support to vulnerable customers. It is true that the UK General Data Protection Regulation (UK GDPR) places a higher standard on certain data types than on others and some vulnerable customer data is captured by the enhanced requirements. It is also just as true that not all vulnerable customer data is subject to this higher standard.

An organisation looking to process data about an individual must always have a lawful basis under UK GDPR to do so. The lawful bases are set out primarily in Articles 6 and 9 of UK GDPR with Article 6 specifying the bases which may be used for 'Personal Data'. Personal data is information such as a person's name, date of birth, address, email address, place of work and financial details such as income, wealth, expenditure, debts and bank account details. This data can be processed for one of the following six reasons:

1. the data subject has given consent to the processing of his or her personal data for one or more specific purposes;

2. processing is necessary for the performance of a contract to which the data subject is party or in order to take steps at the request of the data subject prior to entering into a contract;

3. processing is necessary for compliance with a legal obligation to which the controller is subject;

4. processing is necessary in order to protect the vital interests of the data subject or of another natural person;

5. processing is necessary for the performance of a task carried out in the public interest or in the exercise of official authority vested in the controller;

6. processing is necessary for the purposes of the legitimate interests pursued by the controller or by a third party, except where such interests are overridden by the interests or fundamental rights and freedoms of the data subject which require protection of personal data, in particular where the data subject is a child.

Article 9 of UK GDPR sets out what it calls 'special categories of data' which include, among other fields, data relating to the health of an individual. Where a firm, defined as a Data Controller or Data Processor in UK GDPR, wants to process such data they need both an Article 6 basis (listed above) and an Article 9 basis to do so. The two do not need to be compatible, but the Data Controller must have identified the appropriate basis.

Vulnerability is therefore not always a special category of data; bereavement, job loss, relationship breakdown and financial difficulties, on their own, are examples of vulnerabilities which do not require an Article 9 basis. However, if the vulnerability is related to a health condition or disability, an Article 9 basis will be required as well. Note that if, for example, job loss leads to anxiety, then the anxiety would be a health condition and would require an Article 9 basis.

One basis that may be used under Article 9 is explicit consent. This is the most well-known and used basis for processing special categories of data. It is, after all, the fairest option because it requires the Data Controller (or Processor) to explain to the Data Subject that they are seeking to process the data, explain how they would use the data (i.e. to support the individual) and seek the customer's explicit consent to do so. For the consent to meet the standard of 'explicit' this must be a positive, active statement of consent provided by the Data Subject. It is the fairest basis because not only is the Data Subject aware of what is happening with their data, but they are in full control.

Nevertheless, disclosure does not always work this smoothly. Customers get cut off, become distressed or sometimes can't understand what is being asked of them. Despite this, the customer may have just disclosed a vitally important piece of information relating to their health, one which may impact the way in which the account should be managed, such as when making important investment decisions, or the way in which support is provided to the customer, i.e. support could be tailored to the specific needs of the customer. In these situations, it would be beneficial for the customer service staff to record the vulnerability and provide the support, despite the fact that explicit consent has not been obtained.

Unless the customer can be re-contacted and explicit consent gained, the Data Controller should look towards the other bases in Article 9 to determine if the data can be processed. There are several others, such as data which is necessary for employment law (i.e. health and safety), social protection law, or to protect the vital interests of a person. The latter is strictly limited to situations where the data is needed to keep an individual alive and consent cannot be obtained from the data subject. The basis that is of most interest to financial services firms is in Article 9 (2g) which reads "processing is necessary for reasons of substantial public interest, on the basis of Union or Member State law which shall be proportionate to the aim pursued, respect the essence of the right to data protection and provide for suitable and specific measures to safeguard the fundamental rights and the interests of the data subject;". The Data Protection Act 2018 provides clarity on when Article 9(2g) has been satisfied, Schedule 1, Part 2, paragraph 18 in particular which lists the substantial public interest considerations. One listed is "safeguarding the economic wellbeing of certain individuals". Those certain individuals are individuals who are at economic risk due to their inability to protect their economic situation because of physical or mental illness, injury or disability. Under this section health data may be processed if it is necessary to protect such individuals from economic harm and the following can be satisfied:

- the data subject cannot give consent, or
- the data-controller cannot reasonably be expected to obtain consent, or
- obtaining consent would expose the data subject to harm to their economic wellbeing.

Labelled the 'economic wellbeing' basis, it allows for the capture and use of health data about vulnerable customers where it is processed to protect that individual's financial wellbeing and they are unable to provide consent, it is unreasonable to obtain consent, or obtaining consent would harm them. Essentially it means that consent should be considered in the first instance – after all this is the fairest way to process data – however where consent is not possible then the data can nevertheless be processed. This section began by stating that 'all too often Data Protection is cited as a barrier to providing support to vulnerable customers' and this is due to a lack of understanding around the economic well-being basis, with those who believe explicit consent is the only way to process health data placing unnecessary barriers in the way of capturing data which can be used to support vulnerable customers.

An example which helps to highlight the importance of using a range of bases is where disclosure is received from an unauthorised third party, such as a close friend or relative. In this situation the third party may contact a provider to explain the customer is in poor health and is uncontactable, perhaps due to hospital admission or because they are so unwell they are unable to speak to the provider. Many firms, scared by UK GDPR, would refuse to take the information provided, often also declining to provide support to the affected customer. This position would be a breach of both the Vulnerable Customer Guidance and now the Consumer Duty, because, in reality, the data could be processed under the economic well-being basis. The firm devised its policies to remain GDPR compliant and ended up breaching FCA regulation. Moreover, they failed to record vital information which could be used to support a vulnerable customer and maintain their financial wellbeing.

Let's consider why it is important to process a wide range of vulnerable customer data. Ultimately it is required in order to identify the support best suited to the customer's circumstances. Identifying the appropriate support will sometimes require the vulnerability itself to be identified, recording the condition itself can give important contextual information to agents working on an account, smoothing the conversation, preventing the need for the customer to re-disclose their condition (the need for repeated disclosure was cited by the FCA in the Occasional Paper No.8 as a concern) and, importantly, may impact decisions in relation to support. For example, a firm assisting a customer with stage 2 cancer to plan their financial affairs would benefit from recording the condition as they will need to consider what might happen if the condition worsened. Failing to record the fact that it is cancer, could mean that they were unable to ascertain whether the condition was one that could progress over time.

Supporting customers

Recording the right information at disclosure is the first, vital, step to supporting customers with additional support needs. In the preceding section we highlighted why this is important, we will now consider what is important to record to properly support customers.

Recording both the cause and effect of the customer's vulnerability is, according to the Money Advice Trust, required to be able to ascertain the support needs of the customer. The cause is the condition itself which is an important piece of information in order to provide context, prevent re-disclosure and improve the customer experience. At the point of disclosure, the firm obtaining the information shouldn't solely rely on this, but also seek to understand the 'effect' the vulnerability has on the customer. This is because a central expectation of the FCA is for firms to provide bespoke solutions to vulnerable customers, avoiding generic, cohort-based actions which may cause harm. As such, firms should avoid treating all customers with a specific vulnerability in exactly the same way, for instance, by offering all customers with depression the same solution. Instead, it must be recognised that vulnerabilities impact individuals differently. Depression for Person A may affect their cognitive function, ability to sleep and last for longer than Person B who may experience a completely different set of symptoms. It is the responsibility of the firm receiving the disclosure to conduct conversations with customers in a manner which helps them to detail the effect(s) the vulnerability has on the customer.

Often the support which can then be provided to the customer logically flows from the effect of the vulnerability. Take Person A who may explain to their car finance provider they have depression, motivated to do so because they are unable to work, are receiving a reduced level of income and are therefore unable to maintain payments. The customer services agent thanks the customer for providing that information and explains how the information will be used if they consent for it to be recorded. The agent obtains explicit consent before asking key questions about how their condition impacts them and their ability to manage finances, communicate, and work. It is at this point that the effect will be drawn out and be used to assess solutions and put them in place to support the customer. In this case Person A may well have stated that they have regular bouts of depression, linked to this time of year but it is very debilitating. Because of a lack of sleep they struggle to function or remember key information, but with assistance from a community nurse are usually able to recover in around three months. Now that the company has this detailed information, the most useful support options are clear, the customer would benefit from breathing space and three months without unnecessary contact. After this time the company can check-in with the customer using a 'no pressure' message to ascertain their health at that time.

There are an unlimited array of support options that can be provided. The most common option offered where a debt is owed is breathing space. Under the Debt Respite Scheme (Breathing Space Moratorium and Mental Health Crisis Moratorium) (England & Wales) Regulations 2020 certain debtors have the legal right to 60 days of breathing space ("standard breathing space") where they cannot or are unlikely to be able to repay their debts and are taking advice from a debt advisor. To qualify the debtor must:

a. Be an individual;

b. Owe a qualifying debt;

c. Live or usually reside in England and Wales;

d. Not have a debt relief order, individual voluntary arrangement, interim order or be an undischarged bankrupt at the time that they apply; and

e. Not have had a breathing space in the last 12 months.

Most debts qualify, although some debts are specifically excluded:

- Secured debts (although arrears on these debts may qualify for a breathing space);
- Debts incurred from fraud or fraudulent breach of trust;
- Liability to pay fines imposed by a court for an offence;
- Child maintenance or obligations under an order in family court proceedings;

- Student loans;
- Damages ordered to be paid for death or personal injury; and
- Obligations from a confiscation order.

During the breathing space any enforcement action must be paused, as must collection activity. Additionally, fees, charges and interest cannot be charged during the breathing space period (apart from interest on a secured debt, although not the arrears of that debt).

Where the customer is in what the legislation terms a 'mental health crisis' they are able to request a similar breathing space of the length of time it takes them to recover, plus 30 days under the statute. The qualification criteria are the same as the standard breathing space except the debtor must also be receiving mental health treatment at the time.

There is no limitation on the number of times a customer may use the mental health breathing space in a twelve-month period, whereas the standard breathing space may only be used once every twelve months.

Most FCA regulated firms already had similar protocols in place in relation to providing breathing space as the regulations largely mirror pre-existing requirements in CONC and MCOBS which themselves were taken from industry guidance. Insurance firms will offer a similar level of breathing space in relation to their products where customers are finding it difficult to maintain payments or the firm is collecting payments from customers for other reasons.

The second most common method of supporting customers are adjustments to communication beyond a pause in contact for a period of time. Amending communication largely falls into two categories. The first is simplifying the content of communications which can be a useful solution where the customer's vulnerability makes it difficult for them to choose or understand a service. Difficulty to choose or understand a service is the effect of the vulnerability; the types of vulnerabilities which may cause this effect include learning difficulties, limited experience with financial services, low levels of education or reading age and/or other cognitive disabilities. Simplifying the content of communication can clearly support these customers to make effective decisions.

The second communication adjustment may also be useful to support customers who find it difficult to understand a service, this is to adjust the timing and frequency of communications. The theory is that where information is broken down into bitesize, manageable chunks, it is more understandable for individuals who may otherwise struggle to comprehend the information when it is provided in a single, potentially overwhelming, document. This approach can also be useful where complex statutory information is required to be provided under relevant legislation. Whilst the wording cannot be altered by the firm, additional information such as a cover letter explaining the key aspects of the statutory information is an example provided by the FCA as good practice.

Those offering advisory services will be able to take a more 'hands on approach' where it has been identified that the customer has a vulnerability which makes it difficult for them to comprehend the service. The advisor will need to be well-trained to be able to communicate with the customer in a way which is designed to support their understanding, using less complex terms, providing more time for questions and answers and breaking down information.

Some vulnerabilities make it difficult for customers to access or use a service. Conditions such as blindness is an obvious example, the following may also make access or use difficult for customers: computer illiteracy, autism, and dementia as well as time limited conditions such as depression, anxiety or bi-polar disorder. The solutions in this situation need to be based around accessibility related adjustments and high-quality staff training to provide support where it is apparent that a customer is having difficulty using the service. In FG 22/5 the FCA highlight the need to step outside of usual processes where customers require this type of support, highlighting the benefit of empowering staff to do so.

Firms must also recognise that they won't always be able to offer solutions to customers, this is because some of the effects of a person's vulnerability are outside of the firm's control. Nevertheless, the Consumer Duty places a Duty of care on the firm to signpost the customer to relevant support.

In this section we have given a selection of support mechanisms that can be used to help customers with additional support needs. Such practices are not prescribed under the Consumer Duty, they are, however, cited as good examples in several pieces of the FCA's literature.

In summary, there are three forms of support that can be provided which depend on the effect of the customer's vulnerability. These can be classified as:

1. Things which make a difficult for a customer to choose or understand a service.

2. Things which make it difficult for a customer to access or use a service.

3. Things outside of the firm's control.

Using data

The Duty's requirements in relation to vulnerable customers do not stop at the identification, recording and supporting of individual customers. An echo of the requirement under the Vulnerable Customer Guidance, there is also a need to use vulnerable customer data to improve the service going forward.

Summarised in FG 22/5, the FCA "expect firms to be proactive when evidence emerges that consumers who share protected characteristics are disproportionately experiencing harm or are vulnerable to harm. We expect firms to consider this evidence, review their relevant conduct and assure themselves that they are complying with the requirements of the Duty and obligations under the Equality Act 2010 or equivalent legislation." (FG22/5, p.120)

On a practical level, firms should use the vulnerable customer data they are gathering to analyse the vulnerabilities in their target market, focusing on both the cause and effect of those vulnerabilities. Where certain effects are prevalent, steps can be taken to redesign the product or service to best protect customers from harm. For example, it might be identified that a number of customers find it difficult to provide information over the phone, so a manufacturer may design the service related to the product to include a range of methods of communication, and opening this to all customers not only those who have disclosed vulnerability. The advantage of doing this is that customers who have a similar vulnerability but have not disclosed it are also supported. In turn the manufacturer should see an increase in customers receiving good value, avoiding harm and pursuing their financial objectives. Equally, pressure is likely to be relieved on specialist vulnerable customer teams because contact is no longer required to access support.

Clearly disclosures help to build a data set which can be used positively, however the FCA do highlight the following in FG 22/5:

> "There is a range of ways that firms can gain insight into the experiences and outcomes of customers who share protected characteristics, without requiring their customers to disclose this information. For example, firms could consider the following points.
>
> - They could conduct research into the experiences and needs of a particular group of customers. For example, they could consider focus groups with older customers or a deep dive into their specific needs.

- Working with a consumer organisation that represents a particular group of consumers could help a firm to gain insight into the needs and experiences of that group.

- An audit of customer journeys could identify differences in experience or frictions that affect certain groups of customers but not others.

- Firms could draw on the diversity of their staff. For example, a network of staff with a particular sexual orientation could provide insight into the experiences that this group has when dealing with financial services.

- Firms might be able to use proxy data to infer outcomes experienced by different groups of customers. For example, it may be possible for firms to use customer name and post code as a proxy for ethnicity in certain circumstances. Firms would need to carefully manage any risks and be mindful of their data protection obligations when using proxy data"

(FG22/5, p119)

10.5: Testing and monitoring requirements

Good consumer support, or customer service if you prefer, is unlikely to be provided without first testing the proposed support. Communications used to support customers may be understandable for the professional who created them, but they may not be as understandable for the customer. As a result, testing is an important element of building a support provision which works for customers.

When testing, firms must be conscious to test against the target market(s) their product is designed for, this is confirmed in PRIN 2A.5.12G. This may mean the same communication could be tested several times where a firm has similar products, and therefore similar communications, but designed for different target markets. After all, the Duty is looking through the lens of the customer and their ability to understand rather than the lens of the communication.

Testing of consumer support needs to go beyond the testing of communications to testing of the customer journey focusing on whether friction has worked as intended, the target market is able to access the service as intended and whether the customer perceives any barriers, such as cost, to obtain support.

Good consumer support cannot be provided without monitoring the success of the support provision, using the data to continually improve. Two quotes from the final guidance neatly summarise the regulatory expectations:

> "Firms should regularly monitor whether they are providing an appropriate level of support to customers to identify and mitigate the risk of consumer harm and ensure they meet the standard set out under this outcome. This means that firms must ensure the support they provide enables customers to realise the benefits of products or services and act in their interests without unreasonable barriers, including unreasonable additional costs. This guidance explains when and how these issues may arise but, as explained above, we do not intend to set rigid standards in this area and firms should consider what these terms mean in the context of their business and design systems and processes to monitor this" (FG 22/5, p.105)

> "Firms should produce and regularly review MI on the outcomes they are delivering for customers with characteristics of vulnerability. MI should be of sufficient quality and depth for firms to be able to identify which products and processes are working well, and which might

> be causing detriment and need changing to improve outcomes" (FG22/5, p118)

It is therefore important to ensure the product governance framework picks up appropriate MI addressing the outcomes customers receive, and where outcomes are negative focusing on the root cause to address issues which may derive from the support provision. A range of MI may be used such as customer feedback, complaints or queries which indicate the customer is encountering a barrier, accruing unreasonable costs, or finding the support provision difficult to understand.

If, for example, a firm identifies that a systemic or recurring issue in the delivery of its consumer support prevented customers from utilising a product or service as anticipated, it should act in good faith and consider whether remedial action would be appropriate. This might include providing redress commensurate with the benefit that was difficult to utilise or proactively contacting customers to explain the issue and the steps they can take to fully utilise the product or service

CHAPTER ELEVEN

OUTCOMES MONITORING

11.1: Monitoring Framework

Introduction

One of the more difficult requirements to grasp is the outcomes monitoring requirement under PRIN 2A.9, yet it is vital in order to maintain compliance. Outcomes monitoring has its place in the product governance framework because it is the next logical step following the approval of the product (including ensuring fair value). Following approval, the product or service is distributed in accordance with the arrangements set during the approval stage with the intention of providing customers with positive outcomes. Manufacturers must then continually assess whether they have been successful in achieving this aim.

Scope

It is clear from this section of the Handbook that both manufacturers and distributors are within scope of the outcomes monitoring requirement, although "the monitoring obligation applies proportionately to a firm's role in the distribution chain." (PRIN 2A.9.4G) Therefore it is clear that distributors can generally monitor fewer areas, instead focusing on significant areas of customer harm identified as being within their control. To achieve this, it is often the case that data will be needed from others in the distribution chain, typically the manufacturer, and PRIN 2A.9.4G requires reasonable endeavours are used to share/obtain this information.

PRIN 2A.9

A starting point is to understand the requirements set out in PRIN 2A.9. Whilst this section does not give us a detailed list of monitoring criteria, there is some important guidance located within this section. Firstly, vital context is provided in PRIN 2A.9.2G "*The purpose of the monitoring obligation is to enable firms to identify whether there are any risks that they are not meeting the requirements of the cross-cutting obligations and the retail customer outcomes, and consequently they are not acting to deliver good outcomes for retail customers.*". There are also hints that firms may use data already gathered for other areas of Consumer Duty compliance, see PRIN 2A.9.5 and PRIN 2A.9.7.

The base expectations are to regularly monitor the outcomes that customers are receiving from the products manufactured or distributed, customer support, and communications issued by the firm. (There are specific standards set out in PRIN 2A.5.10R to PRIN 2A.5.14R in relation to the monitoring of communications, these include the need to test communications before launch, and regularly monitoring the impact that the communications are having to identify whether they are supporting good outcomes. Not all communications require testing and monitoring, instead organisations should focus on those designed to prompt the customer to make a decision. Examples include where the decision is important for the outcomes that customers will receive and those directed to customers who, by virtue of their characteristics, require further support, including vulnerable customers and whether, to support good outcomes, the communication required was urgent. When determining whether a communication falls within the testing requirement, a useful test is to assess the level of harm retail customers may experience if they fail to act in accordance with the communication).

PRIN 2A.9.9R explains that outcomes monitoring should enable a firm to determine the following:

1. whether retail customers are being, or have been, sold products that have been designed to meet their needs, characteristics and objectives;

2. whether the products that retail customers purchase provide fair value and appropriate action has been taken to address products identified as not providing fair value;

3. whether retail customers are equipped with the right information to make effective, timely and properly informed decisions; and

4. whether retail customers receive the support they need.

Therefore, all four areas must be included within the design of a firm's outcomes monitoring and it is good practice to frame management information reporting around the same areas. PRIN 2A.9.10R creates an additional measure, which is to assess whether any group of customers receive a different outcome to another. For example, a manufacturer may review, as a group, customers who use the same distribution channel to access the product. It may be identified that customers receive different outcomes, or increased instances of harm, where they have bought the product online rather than with the guidance of a member of the sales team. Firms may also look at repeat customers against new, the age, wealth or experience of customers, and of course those with characteristics of vulnerability.

Action

Where it has been identified that customers receive poorer outcomes than others, including where harm is experienced, action must be taken. Firstly, a root cause analysis (PRIN 2A.9.11R) should be completed and the distribution of products paused until the relevant issues can be resolved. Secondly redress should be considered where it is clear that customers have been harmed due to the product.

Thirdly, organisations must use the results of their monitoring to assess their business model. Business models must be focused on good outcomes; therefore the results of outcomes monitoring must be used to continually review the business model.

A final, but important, action is to report to the Board, at least annually, to confirm whether the firm is producing good outcomes for customers. It is usually at this point that the organisation can review its business model as stated above.

FCA Final Guidance

PRIN 2A.9 is rather light on detail, offering little in the way of substantive guidance. The FCA has provided some further insight into their expectations in FG 22/5 which encourages a focus on the outcomes received by vulnerable customers, identifying whether groups of such customers receive worse outcomes than others. It is clear from their wording that there is an expectation to segment vulnerable customers, rather than simply assess the impact of all customers deemed as vulnerable. Typically, firms may look at those with severe health conditions as one segment, those with vulnerabilities which make it difficult to choose, access or use a service as another, those who may be less likely to understand a product or elements of that product and those with different information needs. Alternatively, particularly for larger firms, grouping vulnerable customers by condition and then further segmenting by effect on the customer could form part of a 'patchwork quilt' approach, ensuring that customers are not receiving different outcomes based on either their named condition or its effect. This is not designed to be an exhaustive list but can act as guidance.

Monitoring should also look beyond vulnerable customers with the final guidance suggesting "Groups that firms could consider might include, for example, longstanding customers, customers from a particular geographical region or customers who buy a product through a particular distribution channel" (FG 22/5).

An excellent barometer of whether organisations are doing enough to measure customer outcomes is whether the same standards are being applied to monitoring *outcomes* as to the monitoring of *sales data*. This also applies to governance reporting, where data provided to committees and management teams should be balanced between outcomes and sales, rather than the traditional approach where reporting would be heavily weighted towards sales and related performance. This meets with the view the regulator has in relation to nature, scale and complexity. Where organisations have more sophisticated data strategies they expect to see more detailed data in relation to outcomes.

The starting point, as set out in the final guidance, is that firms should set a strategy for gathering relevant information and data. Quite often there is an over-reliance on complaints data and whilst this is a useful source of information, clearly outcomes monitoring strategies need to go further. Product usage data can be a good starting point as a data set covering all customers as can business persistence or behavioural insights. However, as stated above, there is an expectation to segment the customer base; file reviews, and distributional analysis using a risk-based approach is an example of the segmentation approach.

Evidence

When a regulated firm creates its monitoring strategy, it must consider information that it may need to produce for the FCA and ensure the evidence is maintained. This is repeatedly referred to in the final guidance, with the following key points:

> "A key part of the Duty is that firms assess, test, understand and are able to evidence the outcomes their customers are receiving."
>
> "If asked, we would expect firms to be able to explain how they reached a decision on the most appropriate intervention, demonstrate how it has delivered good

outcomes and, if not, what they have done further to address the issue."

"We expect firms to [...] be able to demonstrate how they have identified and addressed issues leading to poor outcomes."

"Where a firm considers that distinct groups of customers receiving different outcomes is compatible with the Duty (an example might be when using risk-based pricing) it would need to be able to evidence this to us."

"Firms should also maintain records of the issues that they identify, and the action that they take to address those issues. Firms need to be able to explain how they reached a decision on the right intervention, and to demonstrate how that intervention has delivered better consumer outcomes (and, if not, what they have done further to address the issue)."

"We expect firms to comply with existing FCA rules for record-keeping. For example, our existing record-keeping requirements set an expectation that firms have records that are sufficient to enable us to monitor the firm's compliance with the requirements under the regulatory system."

(FG 22/5).

11.2: Understanding customer behaviour

Perhaps the most useful element of the monitoring section in the final guidance is the examples provided, this allows the reader to achieve a real sense of the regulator's expectations. The examples are:

- Business persistence: analysis of customer retention records – e.g. claims and cancellation rates and details of why customers leave.

This may flag where poor treatment is contributing to high customer turnover.

- Distribution of products/pricing and fees and charges: review of whether certain groups of customers are more likely to buy certain products, incur particular fees and charges, or appear to be receiving outcomes that are not as good as other groups of customers.

- Behavioural insights: customer interactions and drop off rates; use of different communications channels including digital; consumer testing of user interfaces and design such as websites and apps, and the results of such testing, e.g. whether consumers changed their behaviour as a result of the design. This would include consumer testing of any gamification elements in the user interface and design of apps. This may flag where firms need to improve policies, processes and systems (e.g. where there are barriers to consumer engagement or understanding).

- Training and competence records: analysis of records of staff training, including remedial actions where staff knowledge or actions were found to be below expectations.

- File reviews: reviewing customer files and monitoring calls to check for errors and assess if customers received good outcomes (this is particularly useful for sales processes).

- Customer feedback: using formal and informal feedback from customers to identify trends and areas for improvement (e.g. complaints and comments made to the firm but also comments and complaints on social media).

- Numbers of complaints: trends in numbers of complaints involving poor customer outcomes throughout the customer-firm relationship.

- Complaints root cause analysis: investigating complaints fully to understand the cause of customer complaints, not just dealing with the symptoms.

- Results of the regular testing and monitoring required under the outcome rules: many of the four outcomes rules include requirements for firms to monitor and review over time. The results of these reviews, together with any action taken would be relevant for consideration of whether the outcomes are being followed.

- Feedback from other parties in the distribution chain such as manufacturers and distributors sharing information about the way in which products are sold, and the extent to which actual sales matched the target market.

- Compliance reports: review compliance reports to check if standards are being met in terms of good outcomes for consumers.

- Researching or testing customer experiences through processes such as mystery shopping, auditing customer journeys, focus groups and deep dives, or working with consumer organisations to gain insight into the needs and experiences of consumers.

- Allowing staff to feed back honestly when they think products or services, or the processes used to deliver them, could be improved.

- Reviewing whether processes and policies are effective in delivering good outcomes for customers.

- Drawing on external sources of data about consumer outcomes. The Financial Lives survey, for example, contains granular data about the financial lives of different groups.

In respect of vulnerable customers, firms could consider the following points:

- They could conduct research into the experiences and needs of a particular group of customers. For example, they could consider focus groups with older customers or a deep dive into their specific needs.

- Working with a consumer organisation that represents a particular group of consumers could help a firm to gain insight into the needs and experiences of that group.

- An audit of customer journeys could identify differences in experience or frictions that affect certain groups of customers but not others.

- Firms could draw on the diversity of their staff. For example, a network of staff with a particular sexual orientation could provide insight into the experiences that this group has when dealing with financial services.

- Firms might be able to use proxy data to infer outcomes experienced by different groups of customers. For example, it may be possible for firms to use customer name and post code as a proxy for ethnicity in certain circumstances. Firms would need to carefully manage any risks and be mindful of their data protection obligations when using proxy data.

11.3: Taking action

The final guidance also provides suggestions of further actions which may be taken once a problem has been identified, these include:

- adapting, amending or discontinuing a product or service.

- adapting product or service design, fees or charges.
- making appropriate changes to the firm's operations.
- updating customer support processes or distribution channels.
- modifying communications to make them more easily comprehensible.
- providing redress where customers have suffered harm (where appropriate).

Firms are also reminded of their obligations to report serious issues to the regulator. PRIN 2A.9.16G refers manufacturers and distributors to their obligations under the eleventh principle.

11.4: Information sharing

It is not only the FCA with whom findings from outcomes monitoring needs to be shared. Other firms in the distribution chain must also be notified where they or their actions could impact the outcomes of customers relevant to the finding. For example, where, because of outcomes monitoring, a manufacturer changes the process for distributing a product or service, they will need to inform distributors of that product or service of the change. It is also helpful to provide the background reasons for the amended process as this will better equip distributors to train their staff members.

CHAPTER TWELVE

GOVERNANCE AND CULTURE

12.1: Governance Framework

The final element of the product governance framework is reporting to the senior management team. As with any key business process, to be successful the Duty must be led by the top of the organisation with key messages re-enforced and a system of accountability created. For the Consumer Duty the accountability system is the product governance framework. Board reporting is therefore centred around the framework, enabling the board to understand the businesses progress in relation to compliance with the Duty, updates on key actions and most importantly a detailed understanding of the outcomes received by customers. It is the Board's role to drive improvement where gaps are identified and to consider whether the organisation's business strategy is aligned with the Duty, making changes where appropriate.

12.2: Annual Board Report

PRIN 2A.8

The Executive is responsible for implementing the Duty and for its ongoing compliance, and the Board are responsible for challenging and driving the Executive towards the desired culture. This is the overarching message from PRIN 2A.8.

Reporting to the Board must occur at least annually (PRIN 2A.8.3R) and should derive from outcomes monitoring data.

It must:

- Review and approve the firm's report on the outcomes being received by customers.

- Confirm whether it is satisfied that the firm is compliant with the Duty.

- Assess whether the firm's future business strategy is aligned with the Duty.

- Agree actions to remedy any issues identified.

Board Assessment

The Board is essentially assessing whether the firm is compliant with the Duty. It therefore follows that the board should at least consider the content and form of the assessment and ideally formalise their assessment.

The assessment can include:

- the results of the monitoring that the firm has undertaken to assess whether products and services are delivering expected outcomes in line with the Duty, any evidence of poor outcomes, including whether any group of customers is receiving worse outcomes compared to another group, and an evaluation of the impact and the root cause.

- an overview of the actions taken to address any risks or issues.

- how the firm's future business strategy is consistent with acting to deliver good outcomes under the Duty.

Intended outputs

The board are required to ensure that the Duty is appropriately considered at all levels in the organisation, this includes ensuring the

Duty is included and *embedded* in management discussions. Re-enforcing this message should be a key consideration when forming outputs from the board assessment.

A clear action plan, dealing with issues identified from the organisation's product governance framework (outcomes monitoring, product reviews and the board report), must be created and maintained. The action plan must be recorded, actions tracked, and results monitored as part of a system of continuous improvement.

Content of the Board Report

Taking the above contextual information into account, the board report should contain not only the results of outcomes monitoring but qualitative data setting out the root cause of identified issues, such as the impact that remuneration strategies have on customer outcomes.

The level of implementation of the Duty can also be included, assessing whether the product governance framework is functioning but also whether the Duty has been embedded in other areas of the organisation such as second- and third-line checks.

Role of the Board

The role of the board goes beyond the requirement to review and approve the Board report. They are also tasked with promoting the Duty throughout the organisation, communicating the expected standards of conduct, challenging the Executive's actions in relation to implementation of the Duty and benchmarking performance. The FCA state:

> "We expect a firm's board or equivalent governing body to ensure that the Duty is being considered in all relevant contexts, such as considering the impact of their governance and remuneration policies on delivering good outcomes for

> customers and ensuring that customer outcomes are a key lens for risk and internal audit functions." (FG22/5, p.111)

The Board will be supported by a consumer Duty champion, a single individual appointed to ensure that the Duty is raised in relevant discussions and support the chairperson in securing appropriate time at Board meetings to address the report. The FCA state:

> "We expect firms to have a champion at board (or equivalent governing body) level who, along with the Chair and the CEO, ensures that the Duty is being discussed regularly and raised in all relevant discussions. The champion should be an Independent Non-Executive Director (NED), where possible. For larger organisations with group structures, we expect this champion to be at an appropriate level to ensure that the Duty is discussed in a meaningful way. This expectation applies reasonably, so we would not necessarily expect the same level of formality in smaller firms." (FG22/5, p.111)

12.3: Business Model

As highlighted in FG 22/5 an absolute requirement is for the Board to assess whether the firm's business model is compliant with the Duty. There is no exact method of conducting this assessment, therefore it is best demonstrated by an example.

A high-cost-short-term credit provider has developed their MI suite over the last year in accordance with the requirements of the Consumer Duty. This means they have identified data which can be used to assess whether customers are receiving good outcomes, including late payments, arrears, default, switching early from the product and persistent debt (acquiring loans one after another). This together with customer feedback, complaints and employee surveys helps to build a picture of how the product impacts customers. The data is analysed and brought to the annual board meeting where a significant portion of time is given to review it.

Sales related data is also reported at the meeting, presenting a positive picture of the lender's financial standing, they have grown steadily with year-on-year revenues increasing by 20%. However, analysis of the data alongside the MI now obtained for the Duty demonstrates that most of this increased revenue is driven by customers who have repeatedly borrowed from the business, growing their debt month on month and therefore paying significantly more in interest. Analysis of this set of customers identifies those customers borrowing in this way is unsustainable and after four or more loans there is a high risk of default – a negative outcome for both customer and lender. Additionally, the MI demonstrates that around nearly all profit is gained from repeat customers, this is because of the high cost of obtaining new customers making the first loan unprofitable. Understanding this, the business has pushed for previous customers to borrow again through targeted marketing campaigns and special offers.

The Board should step back and look at this situation. The reality of the business' model is that it relies on repeat loans for profitability and customers trapped in a debt cycle for growth. When the board reflect on the financial objectives of their customers, they see that it is to use the service to bridge a short-term financial gap where mainstream finance may not be available. The actual outcomes identified from the MI is not consistent with the objectives of customers, additionally as customers repeatedly borrow, they risk foreseeable harm materialising.

The Board therefore declares that the business model is not consistent with the Duty, proposing a number of changes to remove the reliance on repeat borrowing. They therefore propose to reduce the cost of sale, making the first loan profitable and removing the incentive for the Executive to drive repeat sales. They may also decide to create a second lending proposition, one that is more suitable for long-term borrowing in order to satisfy the demands of those customers who, in reality, need to borrow over the longer term. They build in an assessment during the sales process of both products to check whether the product the customer is purchasing is the best for them. Where it isn't, they are sign-posted to the more suitable product and where customers repeatedly use the high-cost-short-term product, they are moved to the longer-term product. This is an example of a business assessing the needs of customers, alongside the needs of the organisation to form a business model that operates in the interests of all. Each firm falling within the scope of the Duty, no matter what sector, must complete a similar exercise at least every year.

12.4: Culture

Looking back at the high-cost-short-term credit example in our previous section, the Board will (or should) have conducted an exercise to understand all root causes of the poor outcomes received by customers. As highlighted the business model itself was one, however the roots may run deeper.

Culture within the business may be driving a willingness to enable customers to borrow repeatedly in a manner which is detrimental to them. If leaders in the organisation focused mainly on revenue growth and other business focused measures, they may well be driving middle managers to focus on the 'numbers' rather than on the customer. As their success is measured on income growth it is understandable why they may focus on repeat sales as an easy method of satisfying the demands placed on them, especially where the business model didn't enable profitability without doing so. Moreover, perhaps the Executive targeted their middle managers in a way which endorsed this behaviour.

Over time this business-first culture, if left unchallenged, may grow. With staff losing sight of the needs of the individual buying the product, the human behind the numbers and the consequences on those individuals, poor practices can slip into multiple business processes. A focus on reducing the cost of query responses impacting quality is one example. Another is in relation to complaints handling where a dismissive culture can develop from the implied need to put the business first. This implied need can also result in 'play-down' culture where senior managers 'play-down' breaches or issues rather than tackle them. This phenomenon mostly occurs when the issue isn't related to the central goal of the management (revenue growth in our example) but to others, such as customer outcomes. Customer harms can be easily overlooked, especially where managers and the Executive are focused on the wrong data.

Four Drivers

The FCA have helpfully highlighted four key areas organisations should focus on to improve their culture and avoid the traps we have described. The FCA state:

> "Culture is critical to delivering good outcomes for customers. There are four drivers of culture, and firms will need to ensure that acting to deliver good outcomes is central to each.
>
> 1. Purpose – the firm's purpose should be consistent with the Duty. Staff should understand how the firm's purpose is relevant to delivering good outcomes for customers.
>
> 2. Leadership – the firm's leaders should be competent and accountable, and they should demonstrate commitment to delivering good outcomes for customers.
>
> 3. People – delivering good outcomes for customers should be reflected in the way in which people are managed and rewarded. They should be trained to be able to deliver good outcomes for customers.

4. Governance – the firm's controls and key processes should be set up in a way which enables it to identify where the firm is not delivering good outcomes for its customers, and it should have a strategy in place to understand and tackle the root causes and manage and mitigate poor outcomes." (FG 22/5, p.110)

Purpose

We have discussed how a firm's purpose can drive poor culture. The defining factor is where the goals of the organisation overly focus on profit and growth, to the expense of the needs of customers. Equally, it could be detrimental to focus solely on customer outcomes, forgetting about the income, performance and profit businesses do need to survive and grow. Instead, the purpose should be balanced between the two, finding a way to meet both the needs of customers and the financial goals of the organisation.

It is not always easy to define an organisation's purpose, often it will be explicitly stated by the firm's management. It may be found prominently on the firm's website, on posters around the office, lanyards or the desktops of staff. In other cases, the purpose may not be as clearly defined, in which case an important exercise is to observe the workings of the organisation to ascertain what its implied purpose is. Ascertaining the true motivators of staff by reviewing their targets, remuneration structures and feedback they receive can reveal the true purpose of a firm. Looking beyond what senior managers say in public is beneficial too. Look at how they react to information presented to them. Do they 'play-down' issues or, conversely, have they instilled a culture of fear through aggressively blaming individuals when a problem has occurred? Reviewing this and how staff react gives a true view of the purpose of an organisation.

Leadership

Tone from the top is the starting point when building both purpose and culture. By setting out clear expectations staff can go about their duties with confidence they are doing the right thing. The messages given by the leadership do then need to be backed up by actions, as they say "actions speak louder than words". Leaders should set out a clear organisational purpose which balances profit with customer outcomes, supported by values which, amongst others, require individuals to protect vulnerable customers, for example. If staff then make decisions to support vulnerable customers even where there may be a slight cost to the business, but the reaction of senior management is to criticise the decision, focusing solely on the loss of revenue in their reasoning, the value to support vulnerable customers will be lost.

People

A business is nothing without people. Those working throughout the organisation are the ones who impact customers, it is therefore imperative that staff, ranging from frontline staff to senior managers, all work towards the intended culture of the organisation.

People are easily persuaded to modify their behaviour to conform with others around them or to satisfy a person in command, even where they don't morally agree with the actions they are taking. The FCA have recognised this from several examples of non-compliance over the years so understand the importance of influencing people to do the right thing. The factors which influence employees are generally remuneration, rewards, management expectations, targets and the behaviour of others around them. Aligning all of these areas to the intended culture of the organisation is the single biggest factor which influences behaviour and customer outcomes.

Governance

Governance refers to any process, procedure or business action which 'governs' the way in which people work. In other words, it is the work instructions given to staff. Again, these instructions may be explicit in the form of written procedures or implied through accepted ways of working. Regardless of how the instruction is communicated it must be aligned with the intended purpose and culture of the organisation. Careful consideration of the activities which contribute towards the intended outcomes for customers is required prior to creating any such instruction, with competing requirements removed.

Governance also refers to the oversight gained by senior management, essentially one set of the processes and procedures mentioned. The oversight arrangements are imperative to achieving continual review of the success the firm has achieved in implementing its desired culture, of course including good customer outcomes, taking steps to improve at each review. Senior managers will set up a committee structure, with defined agendas and information to be brought to each committee. These will be set out in a 'terms of reference' document for each committee which will also explain the committee's role, responsibilities and outputs. The outputs will be designed to escalate concerns to senior management, this is also an essential part of the Senior Managers and Certification Regime.

CHAPTER THIRTEEN

SENIOR MANAGER RESPONSIBILITIES

13.1: Introduction to SM&CR

The Senior Managers and Certification Regime (SM&CR) was created to mitigate some of the causes of the 2008 financial crisis. Set up in the wake of the crisis, the Parliamentary Commission on Banking Standards criticised the previous accountability regime, the Approved Persons Regime (APR), for two major issues which enabled the environment for the cash to occur.

The first criticism was that the regulator at the time, the Financial Services Authority (FSA), found it difficult to evidence which senior managers were responsible for making decisions for certain areas within regulated firms, specifically those decisions which led to the crash. As a result, the new regime, SM&CR, requires senior managers to maintain a 'Statement of Responsibilities', essentially a list of areas they are responsible for, so the regulator knows the accountable party.

The second criticism was that the APR did not apply widely enough in organisations, it only kept the most senior managers accountable with nothing to oversee the behaviour of middle managers and front-line staff. Save for the lack of statements of responsibilities, the APR's framework was fairly robust in relation to senior management. Senior Managers needed to apply to the regulator prior to undertaking a senior management role in a regulated firm. The regulator would assess their fitness only giving authorisation after they had done so. Once authorised, the individual remained personally liable for failings in their area of control, meaning the regulator could take enforcement action against the individual manager as well as the organisation, including unlimited fines, removal from their role or an outright ban from the industry.

The Senior Managers element of SM&CR is almost the same as that of the APR. Those very senior individuals, essentially the key decision makers in the firm, are personally accountable to the FCA in the way they were under the APR. The only major change is the need to record responsibilities in the Statement of Responsibilities and, for certain firms, the management responsibilities map.

The Certification Regime applies to a set population of staff members depending on their role, this is set out in SYSC 27.8. However, the simplest way to think about the Regime is applying to the next layer of staff working beneath senior management as well as a number of specific roles which means the individual could cause a high risk to customers, firm stability or even sector stability. The FCA's role in relation to the Certification Regime is not as 'hands on' as it is for the Senior Managers Regime, the main difference is that the FCA does not vet applications prior to individuals entering the Certification Regime, instead it is the responsibility of the firm to complete fit and proper assessments. The fit and proper assessment must cover specific criteria, set out in FIT 2.1-2.3. Once assessed the recruiting firm 'certificates' the individual for up to one year and registers them with the FCA. Each year the firm must re-assess the individual's fitness and, if appropriate, recertificate them. The certification regime is designed to create more accountability throughout organisations in a fair and proportionate way.

To ensure that SM&CR was truly transformative, the regulator ensured that an element of the regime applied to nearly all staff members in a regulated firm. There is a small list of ancillary staff members who are outside of the scope of the Regime. SM&CR was designed to improve behaviour in financial services, much the same goal as the Consumer Duty, so it created a number of rules that nearly all staff have to follow. Originally five tier one rules were created, that has now been expanded to six. Tier one rules apply to all staff (save for ancillary staff) whereas tier two rules apply to senior managers as well. Tier one rules include acting with integrity, skill, care and diligence as well as being open and honest with the regulator, treating customers fairly and observing proper standards of market conduct. The newly added sixth rule is to "act to deliver good outcomes for retail customers".

Historically staff were able to conduct poor practice, such as an IFA providing poor advice to customers in order to maximise commission received, and once they were caught, disciplined and dismissed they were often able to move onto work in another organisation, starting with a clean slate. To do so they relied on their previous employer's policy of only providing basic references containing no information about their behaviour. The Regime prevents this from occurring where the person is recruited into a Certification Regime role or a Senior Managers Regime role as the recruiting firm must ask for a 'regulatory reference' from previous regulated employers going back six years. The previous employer is under a duty to include any information relating to a finding the person was not fit and proper, upheld complaints against them or where they have been disciplined due to a breach of the conduct rules and the result of the disciplinary action was a formal written warning or more serious sanction. SM&CR has therefore created a framework whereby people have to live with their actions; this is true accountability.

13.2: SM&CR and the Consumer Duty

The relationship between SM&CR and the Consumer Duty is clear, the Duty is the 'what needs to be done' and SM&CR is the 'who is responsible'. As the FCA state "The SM&CR aims to establish healthy cultures and effective governance in firms by ensuring greater individual accountability at all levels and setting minimum standards of personal conduct." and "The Duty imposes expectations across the product lifecycle including design, distribution and delivery of products and services and each senior manager must take responsibility for the role they can play in delivering compliance with it. Every senior manager should be clear about what they are responsible and accountable for, and how they are ensuring that the business of the firm complies with the requirements of the Duty on an ongoing basis." (FG 22/5, p.113).

Whilst there is not a prescribed responsibility in relation to the Duty, nor is there a requirement to have a specific consumer Duty responsibility in each senior manager's Statement of Responsibilities, it is clear from the final guidance that the expectation is for senior managers to understand their role in delivering products and services which work well for customers and take responsibility for this. The first step is for the senior manager to be clear what they are responsible for, typically the Statement of Responsibilities will be the place to record this. The second step is to evidence the steps taken by the senior manager to discharge their responsibilities effectively.

13.2: Duty of Responsibility

An underappreciated area of FCA regulation is the Duty of responsibility. Section 66A Financial Services and Markets Act 2000 sets out the statutory basis for enforcement action against a senior manager, explaining action may be taken where there has been a failure to comply with the rules of the FCA under section 64A and the individual was a senior manager or approved person of the firm at the time, they were responsible for the management of the area of the business related to the contravention and "the senior manager did not take such steps as a person in the senior manager's position could reasonably be expected to take to avoid the contravention occurring (or continuing)" (https://www.legislation.gov.uk/ukpga/2000/8/section/66A).

It is this final section which provides interesting reading for senior managers, essentially forming a defence to regulatory action where the senior manager can demonstrate they had taken "reasonable steps", despite there being a contravention, such as a breach of the Duty.

To understand what reasonable steps are, the FCA's enforcement manual (DEPP) as well as the conduct rules (tier two) can be examined. DEPP

6.2.9 provides a number of areas the FCA will look at before deciding whether to take enforcement action. This includes whether the senior manager took reasonable steps to understand the regulatory rules impacting the contravention, to delegate activities to individuals who have both the capability and capacity to undertake the activity and, finally, whether the senior manager maintained oversight of the responsibility.

Effectively the regulator is accepting that senior managers will delegate the day-to-day activities under their remit, expecting those they delegate to will maintain compliance with FCA regulations including the Duty. The responsibility given to senior managers is not to ensure the activity occurs in a compliant way but, instead, to manage the delegation reasonably. DEPP and the Conduct Rules provide excellent guidance in this area, including the need to ensure that individuals delegated to are able to carry out those duties, reviewing their competence, capability and capacity. Senior managers should therefore keep records of the CVs, interviews, training and monitoring logs for each subordinate – these may well be required to form a defence to regulatory action in the future. The senior managers role doesn't stop at delegation of course, they also need to oversee the performance of the activity. In this case the senior manager should look to utilise compliance monitoring already undertaken within the organisation as well as other relevant MI already in place, ensuring access to this information and time to analyse the performance of the individual. Taking action where appropriate will help build a comprehensive evidence suite.

Delegation of activities under the Duty are no different, the senior manager must understand the Duty and ensure the governance framework we have described throughout this book is functioning. To do so the senior manager must delegate activities, however they must be careful who to delegate to, ensuring the delegate understands what is required of them and is able to effectively complete their actions. Oversight and constant improvement is then required, just as it is with the Duty itself.

MORE BOOKS BY LAW BRIEF PUBLISHING

A selection of our other titles available now:-

'A Practical Guide to the Independent School Standards – September 2023 Edition' by Sarah McKimm
'A Practical Guide to Estate Administration and Crypto Assets' by Richard Marshall
'A Practical Guide to Managing GDPR Data Subject Access Requests – Second Edition' by Patrick O'Kane
'A Practical Guide to Parental Alienation in Private and Public Law Children Cases' by Sam King QC & Frankie Shama
'Contested Heritage – Removing Art from Land and Historic Buildings' by Richard Harwood QC, Catherine Dobson, David Sawtell
'The Limits of Separate Legal Personality: When Those Running a Company Can Be Held Personally Liable for Losses Caused to Third Parties Outside of the Company' by Dr Mike Wilkinson
'A Practical Guide to Transgender Law' by Robin Moira White & Nicola Newbegin
'A Practical Guide to 'Stranded Spouses' in Family Law' by Mani Singh Basi
'A Practical Guide to Residential Freehold Conveyancing' by Lorraine Richardson
'A Practical Guide to Pensions on Divorce for Lawyers' by Bryan Scant
'A Practical Guide to Challenging Sham Marriage Allegations in Immigration Law' by Priya Solanki
'A Practical Guide to Digital Communications Evidence in Criminal Law' by Sam Willis
'A Practical Guide to Legal Rights in Scotland' by Sarah-Jane Macdonald
'A Practical Guide to New Build Conveyancing' by Paul Sams & Rebecca East
'A Practical Guide to Defending Barristers in Disciplinary Cases' by Marc Beaumont
'A Practical Guide to Inherited Wealth on Divorce' by Hayley Trim
'A Practical Guide to Practice Direction 12J and Domestic Abuse in Private Law Children Proceedings' by Rebecca Cross & Malvika Jaganmohan

'A Practical Guide to Confiscation and Restraint' by Narita Bahra QC, John Carl Townsend, David Winch
'A Practical Guide to the Law of Forests in Scotland' by Philip Buchan
'A Practical Guide to Health and Medical Cases in Immigration Law' by Rebecca Chapman & Miranda Butler
'A Practical Guide to Bad Character Evidence for Criminal Practitioners by Aparna Rao
'A Practical Guide to Extradition Law post-Brexit' by Myles Grandison et al
'A Practical Guide to Hoarding and Mental Health for Housing Lawyers' by Rachel Coyle
'A Practical Guide to Psychiatric Claims in Personal Injury – 2nd Edition' by Liam Ryan
'Stephens on Contractual Indemnities' by Richard Stephens
'A Practical Guide to the EU Succession Regulation' by Richard Frimston
'A Practical Guide to Solicitor and Client Costs – 2nd Edition' by Robin Dunne
'Constructive Dismissal – Practice Pointers and Principles' by Benjimin Burgher
'A Practical Guide to Religion and Belief Discrimination Claims in the Workplace' by Kashif Ali
'A Practical Guide to the Law of Medical Treatment Decisions' by Ben Troke
'Fundamental Dishonesty and QOCS in Personal Injury Proceedings: Law and Practice' by Jake Rowley
'A Practical Guide to the Law in Relation to School Exclusions' by Charlotte Hadfield & Alice de Coverley
'A Practical Guide to Divorce for the Silver Separators' by Karin Walker
'The Right to be Forgotten – The Law and Practical Issues' by Melissa Stock
'A Practical Guide to Planning Law and Rights of Way in National Parks, the Broads and AONBs' by James Maurici QC, James Neill et al
'A Practical Guide to Election Law' by Tom Tabori
'A Practical Guide to the Law in Relation to Surrogacy' by Andrew Powell
'A Practical Guide to Claims Arising from Fatal Accidents – 2nd Edition' by James Patience
'A Practical Guide to the Ownership of Employee Inventions – From Entitlement to Compensation' by James Tumbridge & Ashley Roughton
'A Practical Guide to Asbestos Claims' by Jonathan Owen & Gareth McAloon

'A Practical Guide to Stamp Duty Land Tax in England and Northern Ireland' by Suzanne O'Hara

'A Practical Guide to the Law of Farming Partnerships' by Philip Whitcomb

'Covid-19, Homeworking and the Law – The Essential Guide to Employment and GDPR Issues' by Forbes Solicitors

'Covid-19 and Criminal Law – The Essential Guide' by Ramya Nagesh

'Covid-19 and Family Law in England and Wales – The Essential Guide' by Safda Mahmood

'A Practical Guide to the Law of Unlawful Eviction and Harassment – 2nd Edition' by Stephanie Lovegrove

'Covid-19, Brexit and the Law of Commercial Leases – The Essential Guide' by Mark Shelton

'A Practical Guide to Costs in Personal Injury Claims – 2nd Edition' by Matthew Hoe

'A Practical Guide to the General Data Protection Regulation (GDPR) – 2nd Edition' by Keith Markham

'Ellis on Credit Hire – Sixth Edition' by Aidan Ellis & Tim Kevan

'A Practical Guide to Working with Litigants in Person and McKenzie Friends in Family Cases' by Stuart Barlow

'Protecting Unregistered Brands: A Practical Guide to the Law of Passing Off' by Lorna Brazell

'A Practical Guide to Secondary Liability and Joint Enterprise Post-Jogee' by Joanne Cecil & James Mehigan

'A Practical Guide to the Pre-Action RTA Claims Protocol for Personal Injury Lawyers' by Antonia Ford

'A Practical Guide to Neighbour Disputes and the Law' by Alexander Walsh

'A Practical Guide to Forfeiture of Leases' by Mark Shelton

'A Practical Guide to Coercive Control for Legal Practitioners and Victims' by Rachel Horman

'A Practical Guide to the Law of Driverless Cars – Second Edition' by Alex Glassbrook, Emma Northey & Scarlett Milligan

'A Practical Guide to TOLATA Claims' by Greg Williams

'A Practical Guide to Elderly Law – 2nd Edition' by Justin Patten

'A Practical Guide to Responding to Housing Disrepair and Unfitness Claims' by Iain Wightwick

‘A Practical Guide to the Law of Bullying and Harassment in the Workplace’ by Philip Hyland

‘How to Be a Freelance Solicitor: A Practical Guide to the SRA-Regulated Freelance Solicitor Model’ by Paul Bennett

‘A Practical Guide to Prison Injury Claims’ by Malcolm Johnson

‘A Practical Guide to the Small Claims Track – 2nd Edition’ by Dominic Bright

‘A Practical Guide to Advising Clients at the Police Station’ by Colin Stephen McKeown-Beaumont

‘A Practical Guide to Antisocial Behaviour Injunctions’ by Iain Wightwick

‘Practical Mediation: A Guide for Mediators, Advocates, Advisers, Lawyers, and Students in Civil, Commercial, Business, Property, Workplace, and Employment Cases’ by Jonathan Dingle with John Sephton

‘The Mini-Pupillage Workbook’ by David Boyle

‘A Practical Guide to Crofting Law’ by Brian Inkster

‘A Practical Guide to the Law of Domain Names and Cybersquatting’ by Andrew Clemson

‘A Practical Guide to the Law of Gender Pay Gap Reporting’ by Harini Iyengar

‘NHS Whistleblowing and the Law’ by Joseph England

‘Employment Law and the Gig Economy’ by Nigel Mackay & Annie Powell

‘A Practical Guide to Noise Induced Hearing Loss (NIHL) Claims’ by Andrew Mckie, Ian Skeate, Gareth McAloon

‘An Introduction to Beauty Negligence Claims – A Practical Guide for the Personal Injury Practitioner’ by Greg Almond

‘Intercompany Agreements for Transfer Pricing Compliance’ by Paul Sutton

‘Zen and the Art of Mediation’ by Martin Plowman

‘A Practical Guide to the SRA Principles, Individual and Law Firm Codes of Conduct 2019 – What Every Law Firm Needs to Know’ by Paul Bennett

‘A Practical Guide to Adoption for Family Lawyers’ by Graham Pegg

‘A Practical Guide to Industrial Disease Claims’ by Andrew Mckie & Ian Skeate

‘A Practical Guide to Conducting a Sheriff Court Proof’ by Andrew Stevenson

‘A Practical Guide to Vicarious Liability’ by Mariel Irvine

‘A Practical Guide to Applications for Landlord’s Consent and Variation of Leases’ by Mark Shelton

‘A Practical Guide to Relief from Sanctions Post-Mitchell and Denton’ by Peter Causton

'A Practical Guide to Equity Release for Advisors' by Paul Sams
'A Practical Guide to Financial Services Claims' by Chris Hegarty
'The Law of Houses in Multiple Occupation: A Practical Guide to HMO Proceedings' by Julian Hunt
'Occupiers, Highways and Defective Premises Claims: A Practical Guide Post-Jackson – 2nd Edition' by Andrew Mckie
'A Practical Guide to Financial Ombudsman Service Claims' by Adam Temple & Robert Scrivenor
'A Practical Guide to Running Housing Disrepair and Cavity Wall Claims: 2nd Edition' by Andrew Mckie & Ian Skeate
'A Practical Guide to Holiday Sickness Claims – 2nd Edition' by Andrew Mckie & Ian Skeate
'Arguments and Tactics for Personal Injury and Clinical Negligence Claims' by Dorian Williams
'A Practical Guide to Drone Law' by Rufus Ballaster, Andrew Firman, Eleanor Clot
'A Practical Guide to Compliance for Personal Injury Firms Working With Claims Management Companies' by Paul Bennett
'RTA Allegations of Fraud in a Post-Jackson Era: The Handbook – 2nd Edition' by Andrew Mckie
'RTA Personal Injury Claims: A Practical Guide Post-Jackson' by Andrew Mckie
'On Experts: CPR35 for Lawyers and Experts' by David Boyle
'An Introduction to Personal Injury Law' by David Boyle

These books and more are available to order online direct from the publisher at www.lawbriefpublishing.com, where you can also read free sample chapters. For any queries, contact us on 0844 587 2383 or mail@lawbriefpublishing.com.

Our books are also usually in stock at www.amazon.co.uk with free next day delivery for Prime members, and at good legal bookshops such as Wildy & Sons.

We are regularly launching new books in our series of practical day-to-day practitioners' guides. Visit our website and join our free newsletter to be kept informed and to receive special offers, free chapters, etc.

You can also follow us on Twitter at www.twitter.com/lawbriefpub.

www.ingramcontent.com/pod-product-compliance
Lightning Source LLC
LaVergne TN
LVHW022036200926
848481LV00003B/706